MW00939793

Very informative. Another valua
that every Legal Nurse Consulta
reference to develop a successfu

KATHY A. CARROLL RN BSN CLNC ALNC

*Thank you for another informative and much needed book.
The information is appropriate for Legal Nurse Consultants/
Life Care Planners at any stage in their businesses. I appreciate that Pat addresses how to attain success both as an
LNC and a business owner. Pat discusses financial matters
from setting your fees to maintaining a healthy cash flow for
your business. Thanks to Pat for always sharing her knowledge and giving us such sage advice!*

DIANA BOWEN-GOLDSTEIN RN BSN CLNC

*Starting a legal nurse consultant business is fun and excit-
ing, but very challenging for me, because as a nurse I didn't
know much about running a business. This book helps to
prepare and groom you into a successful entrepreneur. It
provided useful tips and the do's and don'ts of running a
business. It also provided advice on developing an entrepreneurial mindset, how to tackle limiting beliefs, taking care
of your health and wellness, and finding joy and confidence
to become a successful LNC. This book is a must have for
all new and seasoned LNCs. I really enjoyed reading this
book. Pat Iyer is one of the most intelligent, highly recognized, influential legal nurse consultants I know. Thank you,
Pat for yet another awesome and informative book!*

KIM BROWNE, RN, BSN, LNC, CM

I have purchased several of Pat's legal nurse consulting books. I have found all of her books to be very informative and they provide a wealth of information for legal nurses. Pat is truly the expert in the field of legal nurse consulting which is demonstrated by her knowledge and compassion for the field. Pat provides excellent tips and advice for legal nurse consultants. I highly recommend this book!

RUTH HOSTLER RN, MSN, AOCN, CLNC

How to be a Successful Legal Nurse Consultant: Tips for Your Business

Book 9 in the "Creating a Successful LNC Practice" Series

Patricia W. Iyer, MSN RN LNCC

The Pat Iyer Group
Fort Myers, FL

Copyright

How to be a Successful Legal Nurse Consultant: Tips for Your Business

Disclaimer

ISBN-13: 978-1985722422

Also by Pat Iyer

Creating A Successful Legal Nurse Consulting Practice Series:

How to Manage Your LNC Business: Top Tips for Success (Book 8)

How to Grow Your LNC Business: Secrets of Success (Book 7)

How to Get More Cases: Marketing Secrets for LNCs (Book 6)

How to Get More Clients: Sales Secrets for LNCs (Book 5)

How to be a Successful Expert Witness (Book 4)

How to Analyze Medical Records: A Primer for LNCs (Book 3)

Legal Nurse Consultant Marketing (Book 2)

How to Start a Legal Nurse Consulting Practice (Book 1)

Path to Legal Nurse Consulting: Collective Wisdom of Successful LNCs, Second Edition

Analyzing Emergency Department Medical Malpractice Cases

Analyzing Falls, Pressure Sores and IV Therapy Cases

Honing Your Legal Nurse Consulting Practice

Building Blocks of a Legal Nurse Consulting Business

Secrets of Growing Your Legal Nurse Consulting Business

How to Get Published

Safeguard your Ambulatory Care Nursing Practice

Social Media Marketing for Legal Professionals

Iyer, P., Levin, B., Ashton, K. and Powell, V. (Editors), Nursing Malpractice, Fourth Edition,

Iyer, P. and Levin, B. (Editors), Medical Legal Aspects of Medical Records, Second Edition

Legal Nurse Consultants' Handbook

Gray-Micelli, D., Capezuti, E., Lawson, W. and Iyer, P., Falls Handbook: From Public to Patient Settings: Clinical and Medical-Legal Perspectives of Falls Across the Lifespan

Iyer, P. Nursing Home Litigation: Investigation and Case Preparation

Iyer, P., Aken, J. and Condon, K. (Editors), Business Principles of Legal Nurse Consulting

Iyer, P. and Camp, N., Nursing Documentation: A Nursing Process Approach

Medical Legal Aspects of Pain and Suffering, Tucson, AZ, Lawyers and Judges Publishing Company

Principles and Practices of Legal Nurse Consulting, Second Edition

Barbacci, M., Browsky, D., Calderone, A., Cantwell-Davis, S., Clark, K., Iyer, P., Essentials of Medical Record Analysis

Iyer, P., Taptich, B. and Bernocchi-Losey, D., Nursing Process and Nursing Diagnosis,

Taptich, B., Iyer, P. and Bernocchi-Losey, D., Nursing Diagnosis and Care Planning,

Rowland, L. and Iyer, P. (Editor), Patient Outcomes in Maternal Child Nursing

Camp, N. and Iyer, P. (Editor), Patient Outcomes in Medical Surgical Nursing

Whitis, G. and Iyer, P. (Editor), Patient Outcomes in Pediatric Nursing

About the Author

Patricia W. Iyer, MSN RN LNCC

President, The Pat Iyer Group,
Fort Myers, FL

www.legalnursebusiness.com

Pat helps legal nurse consultants get more cases, make more money and avoid expensive mistakes through her coaching program, **www.LNCAcademy.com**. She is a trusted advisor to LNCs. In 1987, Pat began a 20-year career testifying as an expert witness. She created an independent LNC business, Med League Support Services, Inc, which she sold in 2015. Med League provides legal nurse consulting services to personal injury, malpractice, and product liability attorneys.

Pat is a well-known and respected legal nurse consultant. She served for five years on the Board of Directors of the American Association of Legal Nurse Consultants, including a term as national president. Pat was the chief editor of the *Legal Nurse Consulting: Principles and Practices, Second Edition*, the core curriculum for legal nurse consulting and *Business Principles for Legal Nurse Consultants*. She also worked with her team of coeditors when she was the chief editor of the first version of AALNC's LNC Online Course, which teaches nurses how to get started as legal nurse consultants.

Pat is certified as a legal nurse consultant by the American Association of Legal Nurse Consultants. AALNC awarded her with the Lifetime Achievement/Distinguished Service Award and with the Volunteer of the Year Award.

A prolific author, Pat has written, edited or coauthored over 800 articles, chapters, case studies, webinars, and online courses on a wide variety of nursing topics.

The creator of the first legal nurse consulting podcast show, Pat launched a twice weekly podcast called Legal Nurse Podcasts, available on ITunes and **podcast.legalnursebusiness.com**.

Pat shares her expertise with LNCs through books and on-line training available on **www.LegalNurseBusiness.com**. She provides monthly online training at **LNCEU.com**.

Learn successful business strategies at **http://lnc.tips/5Surefire**.

Pat works with LNCs who want to get more clients, make more money and avoid expensive mistakes. When you are ready to make a financial and emotional commitment to growing your business, check out **http://LNCAcademy.com**. Let's work together to make your dreams come true.

Reach Pat at **patiyer@legalnursebusiness.com**

Client Testimonials

If you are a legal nurse consultant and you want to build a business as a legal nurse consultant you definitely need to look into the work that Pat Iyer does and get in touch her and work with her because she can help you. She can coach you and she will get you to the success you deserve, and your business deserves. There are a lot of entrepreneurs who start their business and fail because they never worked with a coach. And not any coach, a coach who has already done the things you want to achieve. Pat has achieved amazing things in her legal nurse consulting business.

IMAN AGHAY

I joined Pat's LNC Academy about a year ago. In the last year I have grown my business, and I have grown my understanding of the business in leaps and bounds. I think Pat is a wonderful mentor. She's made all the difference to me and my business. I definitely recommend if you're considering joining to do it. You won't regret it and it will help your business.

SANDRA KRUG

The services you provide are invaluable and you are one to look up to.

REBECCA M. BLEVINS

I've been a member of Pat Iyer's LNC Academy for a year and I'm planning to renew my membership next year. Through Pat's coaching I've developed a successful professional business image. I've honed my writing skills. I've learned to do video presentations and I've learned to use full marketing skills. I highly recommend the LNC Academy to anyone who wants a successful LNC business. Do you want to boost your LNC business? Check out the coaching programs Pat Iyer offers at LNCAcademy.com.

BONNIE O'HARA

I have been a Legal Nurse for a while, and I have been doing a pretty good job at marketing, but I felt lost because I am a nurse. Since attending Pat's webinars, I have enhanced my confidence and marketing knowledge.

RITA BUETTNER

You send us SUCH good info every week! I always look forward to reading your ezines and other information you email out. Thanks so much for ALL you do for us! You keep me inspired about being an LNC!

MARY WILSON, BSN, RN, PLNC, CRRN, CCM

A very knowledgeable, clear and succinct presentation. Pat is also very personable and generous in sharing her expertise.

JOY VINCENT

I have enjoyed every opportunity to learn from Pat Iyer. Her seasoned experience in the field of legal nurse consulting is impressive and humbles me each time I consult with her. She is flexible, responsive, grounded, ethical and sound with her advice. Thank you Pat for each collegial opportunity!

GINA M. D'ANGELO RN BSN MBA NHA CLNC RAC-CT

Thank you for laying the groundwork for people like me.

SONDRA RUTMAN RN BA LNC

I am very grateful for all you have taught me. There is no way I would be working inhouse as an LNC if not for you. I really feel good about myself getting dressed professionally and going to work among people who respect what I have to say.

ILENE SCHWARTZ

I sure enjoy reading your articles with all the tips included. I'm always up for learning new tips and strategies.

CHRISTINA FREEDAN

I was overwhelmed with so much I realized that needed to be done. With Pat's help and the discussions with the other nurses about subcontracting on our LNC Academy Q&A call, I learned so much that will help my business grow. I learned how to improve my case analysis and report writing. And this is only the tip of the iceberg.

DEBBIE WUERL

The CT Chapter of the American Association of Legal Nurse Consultants was fortunate recently to have Pat Iyer agree to present the webinar, "From Cold Calls to Hot Prospects: How to Build Your Client Base" to our chapter membership. Pat is a strong presenter and presents in a comprehensive and clear manner. Pat included information pertinent to legal nurse consultants promoting their practices in CT, which was an unexpected surprise. Feedback for her webinar has been overwhelmingly positive. I highly suggest Pat as an instructor and presenter to both new and experienced legal nurse consultants.

LORRAINE DOONAN, RN, BSN, MS, CPHQ, LNCC, CSA

Pat Iyer has so much expertise to share. I see a sincere desire to help LNCs succeed.

SUSAN KLEVANS

Acknowledgements

The author appreciates the contributions of these people to the material in this book.

Lisa Brown - **Lisabrownpresents.com**

Belanie Dishong - **Liveatchoice.com**

Bonnie Fatio - **Ageesteem.com**

Dorci Hill - **Dorcihillglobal.com**

John Kriger - **Techdependence.com**

Marcey Rader - **Marceyrader.com**

Joy Marsden - **Joymarsden.com**

Lori Rochino - **Lorirochino.com**

Debbie Lyn Toomey - **Healthandhappinessspecialist.com**

Dartrice White - **dawhite.net**

Contents

Introduction

Are you interested in a successful LNC business? I am assuming you are or otherwise you would not be here with me.

I've learned the success of LNCs is based on several factors that I describe in this book. I've shared with you the success principles that I know lead to successful businesses whether you are a legal nurse consultant or life care planner.

This book has 3 sections: what makes you successful, what makes your business shine, and what goes on in your mind to influence success. Launching a successful marketing campaign is great, but you need to be able to manage the business that comes in and make smart business decisions.

In this book, I reveal secrets of what I learned from running a very successful LNC business. By applying this knowledge, you are a head start in running your business.

The book you are holding is the ninth book in a series I began in 2016, named **Creating a Successful LNC Practice**. This series is designed to give you the essential knowledge you need to grow your business.

Book 1 in the **Creating a Successful LNC Practice Series** is *How to Start a Legal Nurse Consulting Business*. It takes you from the point when you leave your LNC training program and enter the world of becoming a business owner. You will learn how to develop the mindset and attitudes that allow entrepreneurs to thrive. I cover how to set up and manage your business, track your finances, get your first case and create a professional image that attracts clients to you. You will get tips on how to reach out to attorneys and work your network. This book is ideal for both the new and more experienced LNC business owner.

Book 2 is *Legal Nurse Consultant Marketing*. This is a comprehensive compilation of tips, techniques and technology. You will explore how to develop your marketing plan and website, and to share your expertise to attract attorneys to you. Presenting at attorney conferences or law firms involves skills you will learn in this book. You will find out how to harness the power of video by creating videos that highlight your skills.

Unsure about how to close the deal? The chapter on sales walks you through the process of bringing the case in. You will discover techniques to become more persuasive in your marketing. Take advantage of the two chapters on exhibiting to crack the code on one of the most successful ways to meet attorneys to build a customer base. I wrapped the book up with a chapter that answers common marketing questions. This book has something for LNCs with all levels of experience, from new to more seasoned.

Book 3 is called *How to Analyze Medical Records: A Primer for Legal Nurse Consultants*. Use it to get tips and techniques for organizing paper and electronic medical records, the backbone of our business. You will gain an understanding of how to screen a medical malpractice case for merit and discover clues for detecting tampering with medical records. The book covers the pros and cons of electronic medical records, including how they introduce risk into the documentation of patient care. Two final chapters focus on how to polish your work product to create your strongest professional appearance. You will gain critical insights on how to strengthen your ability to analyze medical records – to gain more clients and earn more money.

Book 4 is *How to be a Successful Expert Witness.* Written for the healthcare expert witness, it is based on my more than 25 years of testifying as an expert witness. In this book, I share tips on how to get cases as an expert, how to polish your CV, and how to master report writing and testifying. Use this book to increase your confidence and skills in what is a challenging aspect of litigation.

Book 5 is *How to Get More Clients: Marketing Secrets for Legal Nurse Consultants.* This comprehensive book prepares you to take advantage of a range of ways to market your business. I share concepts relating to branding, relationship marketing, online marketing and more. You will discover techniques to help prospects and clients know, like and trust you. You will get in-depth knowledge of using websites and social media to market. Legal nurse consulting is particularly rich in stories. One section of the book defines the power of stories in attracting clients

– whether those stories relate to cases you've handled or are the testimonials you collect from clients. Exhibiting provides a great opportunity to meet your prospects face to face. I built my business with exhibiting. The last section provides solid tips for what you need to know to have a successful exhibiting experience.

How to Get More Cases: Sales Secrets for Legal Nurse Consultants is Book 6. Marketing brings the attorney to your door. Sales enables you to bring the case through your door. Your ability to fine tune your sales approach makes the difference between success and failure. You'll discover how your personality affects sales, and how to successfully sell to attorneys. I share secrets of warming up cold prospects and making a dynamite presentation during a sales opportunity. Finally, you will get tips for closing the sale.

How to Grow Your LNC Business: Secrets of Success is Book 7. This book focuses on growth – the factors that help your business expand. First, consider your mindset – are you your friend or enemy? Then, take the opportunity to make presentations to attorneys to demonstrate your skills. And then learn from the success stories of LNCs.

Book 8 is *How to Manage Your LNC Business and Clients*. You've gotten started, you've gotten clients, and you want to sustain your success. Business development and client management are intertwined. Both are necessary for a stable business. In this book I tackled how to control your money and your goals, to subdue the evil twins of perfectionism and procrastination, and to get more done through outsourcing. You can reach a stressed out state as a business owner. I share tips for managing your stress and health. Ready to hire an employee? I added a chapter on the process of interviewing and hiring. The second part of the book shares tools and techniques for deepening your relationships with your clients. You will discover how to win over and retain the clients you want and recognize those who are too much trouble. Mastering negotiation, business communication and conflict are essential. I show you how. This is the book to use to build a stable foundation for your business.

Invest in these books at **www.legalnursebusiness.com**. Send me your comments and suggestions at patiyer@legalnursebusiness.com.

Part 1:

Your Success

Chapter 1

Building a Successful LNC or Life Care Planning Business

Legal nurse consultants ask me about what I did to create such a successful independent legal nurse consulting practice. I followed some principles that foster success. Your definition of a successful LNC business may be different than mine. When I sold my LNC business, I was billing more than a million dollars a year for the last 5 years I owned the company.

Here's what I learned that you may find useful.

1. If possible, create your business launch so that you are not under pressure to make a profit right away. It takes more time than you would expect to market and start attracting clients. When I started Med League, my husband was bringing in enough money that I could take my time and be self-employed through teaching nurses, consulting with hospitals, and doing expert witness work. Gradually I centered on working with attorneys as my primary source of business activity.

2. Learn the nuances of marketing and writing appealing copy for brochures and websites. Your prospect is bombarded with information. You must capture that person's attention quickly and in a compelling way. I have studied this aspect of running a business and invested thousands of dollars in courses, mentors, and books to learn more about marketing. The more you understand about marketing, the more comfortable and confident you feel.

3. Pick the right service that fits your strengths. If you have a broad base of nursing, you are in an ideal position to help attorneys understand nursing malpractice cases. If you have worked only critical care, and continue to maintain a clinical practice, you may be in an ideal position to testify as an expert witness on critical care cases. Know what you are good at and recognize it cannot be all aspects of running a business. Find others to help you where you are weak.

Recognize that you need a solid foundation in clinical nursing to be able to work most effectively with attorneys. I worked on medical surgical units as a staff nurse for years before I took my first expert witness case. Understanding how a hospital runs is invaluable in assisting attorneys. Nurses who have experience only in non-hospital roles are going to find it tougher to perform some aspects of legal nurse consulting.

4. Be aware of the advantages and disadvantages of working on cases or for attorneys who could swamp your firm with volume. For example, a multidistrict litigation case could become the elephant that pushes out the time you have to attorneys who send you one case at a time. When we worked on pedicle plates and screws cases, our regular clients noticed the longer turnaround for their cases. We were on a continuous treadmill of churning out reports and were relieved when the cases finally wound down.

5. **Never stop marketing** and don't rely on only one client for work. Your primary client could have a sudden change in practice due to a change in the law, or could leave the firm, or drop dead. In my husband's case, one year he got 90% of his income from one client. (He sold machine parts.) Disaster struck when that client figured out a way to cut him out of the deal. My husband lost his entire business overnight and for the next year, struggled to make any money at all. I learned from that experience.

At one point I got 30% of my income from one large personal injury law firm. It would have been tempting to sit back and relax, but I never stopped marketing, exhibiting, and writing to attract more clients. When the personal injury cases in our state took a nose dive because of changes in the law, my business would have also taken a similar nose dive if I had relied only on this firm for paying the bills.

6. **Consider the multiple ways you can reach your market:** a website, a blog, tweets, Facebook, ezines, emails, videos, and video testimonials. Use these methods to remind your client base of your existence. Use principles

of crafting effective marketing messages and consistently implement them.

7. Do subcontracting work for other LNCs if it makes sense for you in your phase of business development. It will make sense for you if you can afford to work at a rate that will be considerably lower than the rate you would charge the attorney client.

It will also make sense if you need experience and the feedback from a more seasoned LNC. You can be mentored so that you can really understand how to perfect your craft.

8. Get a business coach. Ask yourself, "What would I know about running a business being a nurse?" A business coach knows how to run a business and will guide you with success tips for your LNC business. Your coach may push you way past your comfort zone to help you achieve success. Select an experienced LNC business coach to get the maximum benefit from someone who has been successful. Check out my coaching program at **LNCAcademy.com**.

9. Get Adobe Acrobat Pro so that you can more easily analyze and work with medical records. Although CaseMap is a great program for creating chronologies, in my opinion, you can start with MS Word and invest in CaseMap later in your business. Develop a knowledge of Excel, which can be very useful for creating graphs and tallying numbers.

10. Go to places where you will meet attorneys – bar association events, Chamber of Commerce events, and so on. Be deliberate in your networking by asking questions to identify the people present who handle cases with medical issues. Have plenty of business cards in pockets, your wallet and other easily accessible places.

Attorneys like to meet the people they will be working with – getting out of your house and into their midst is one of the biggest success tips for your LNC business.

11. Work on your mindset, which is part of the benefit of working with a business coach. If I am positive, I really attract positive people in my life. People appreciate working with someone who is positive.

Even if I'm having a negative day if someone says, "How are you doing" I say, "Excellent" because why wouldn't I? Negative people reinforce whatever doubts that you have about your business or your capabilities and can really shoot you way down. Some people never recover from that.

12. Pay attention to relationships. Your clients want to work with people they know, like and trust. Look for ways to build strong relationships with your clients so that they would not dream of working with another person. Advise them when you come across a case like theirs that has been settled or tried and share the result. Be flexible when possible with payment plans. One client of ours was frank with us years ago that his client was responsible for the fees and could not pay the bill, nor could the attorney. Our client told us, "Be flexible with me and I'll make it up to you." He was a loyal client for more than a decade and paid his bills.

13. Leverage your time and talent. You will build a stronger legal nurse consulting practice if you use subcontractors. Hire people who have particular expertise in an area you lack, such as a different type of clinical nursing, to review cases for you. This is a better use of your time than to try to master the nuances of a different area of nursing. Without subcontractors, your income will be dependent on the number of hours you can work.

In 1989, I got a call from an attorney who wanted me to review an emergency department case as an expert. I told him I was not an ED nurse, but knew one who would be excellent for his case. After I connected them, I realized they would both benefit from the introduction, but I had just done a lovely unpaid favor. This was the impetus for forming Med League and recruiting a pool of nursing expert witnesses.

14. Train your subcontractors well. Explain your expectations, give them sample work product, review their samples, and be quick to correct and reject those who are not capable of doing the work. I recall getting a phone call from an attorney who told me my expert had poor grammar and spelling skills. At that time, I did not have a policy in place to proofread our experts' reports. I was horrified by what I saw. We quickly started a proofreading policy which has saved much embarrassment over the years. It helps us evaluate and strengthen the skills of our experts.

15. Use honest and ethical business practices. Return unused portions of retainers, keep detailed billing records, and always check for a conflict of interest before accepting a case. A legal vendor I know told me that she only returns unused portions of a retainer if the client asks for them. That strikes me as dishonest. You must be able to look yourself in the mirror and be proud of your ethics. Your clients will respect you for being ethical.

16. Avoid borrowing money if you can. Use your revenues, not loans, to invest in your business, such as upgrading your computer equipment. When my husband started his welding business in 1980, we borrowed a million dollars and signed personal guarantees for the amount. When his business failed two years later, we were on the hook for a million that we did not have. I was pregnant with our second child when the man came to evaluate our house to determine if it was worthwhile taking to satisfy some of the debt. My husband's keen negotiating skills kept us from having to declare bankruptcy. My LNC business never took a loan since its inception because of our brush with bankruptcy.

17. Charge reasonable fees that the market will bear. Do not join the rush to the bottom to undercut your competitors. You will destroy your business by performing work at the lowest rate on the market, find it impossible to raise fees, and run out of money.

One man called me a few years ago to ask if I wanted to bid on doing medical summaries. He quoted a price he had heard from other companies, which was half of our hourly rate, and asked if I could do better. I wanted to ask him, "Do better for ourselves or for you?" I explained we could not do the work for that rate. Another firm asked us to work on pharmaceutical product liability cases and wait until the cases settled to get paid. I explained we could not ask our subcontractors to wait to get paid; I was unwilling to go into debt to pay them before we got paid. Think through the financial consequences of taking these kinds of arrangements.

18. Charge rush fees. Determine what will constitute a rush rate, with a specific time frame, and adhere to that rate. We charge our clients and pay our nursing expert witnesses a rush rate when they are expected to produce work on a short turn around. I resisted rush rates for years, fearing it would cause us to lose business. I found attorneys expected it, and even volunteered at times, "If you have to, charge me more to get this done."

19. "Hire slowly, fire quickly." There is a great deal of wisdom in that expression. Carefully screen employees. A typo on a resume is enough for me to set it aside. I have fired employees for absenteeism, incompetence, and poor attitude. Be grateful when a marginal employee quits. Although it causes short term disruption, it is far better for a person to self-select out of your system. Don't tolerate marginal work performance. There are far better people looking for work.

20. Use financial and security controls in your business. Avoid providing embezzlement and theft opportunities. Allow only extremely trustworthy employees to access bank accounts. (One of my colleagues caught an employee of a business she owned buying a personal computer charged to the company credit card. The employee counted on the owner not looking at the credit card bill. It was a fluke that the owner saw the bill and caught the purchase.)

Be very careful about allowing employees to remotely access your server. Someone could access a laptop or desktop computer in an employee's home and gain access to your company data. And if that employee quits or gets fired, how will you retrieve your data?

21. Your employees are not your friends. Do not be overly generous. Be fair, be aware of the labor laws, and be careful with benefits and bonuses. Our practice of giving an extra $100 at Christmas over the years became an extra week of pay, and then an extra two weeks of pay. I thought the employees understood this was optional on our part. When 2008 came and we were unable to provide that extra paycheck, it destroyed the morale of my two long term employees. My practice of giving extra and helping my employees on a personal level backfired.

22. Do not allow others to dictate the terms of your business to you. In many cases, LNCs simply do not realize how much control they have over their own business.

If you want to be successful, then you need to get in the habit of taking control and not allowing others to dictate the terms of your business to you. I advocate listening to your clients, but not allowing the disgruntled ones to dictate business practices that would subvert a successful independent legal nurse consulting practice.

For example, when I supplied expert witnesses who worked under contract for me, one of my clients wanted to know how much I paid her. When I asked him why he wanted to know that, he said, "So I can pay her directly and not have to go through you." I politely told him what I paid her was not his business.

Attorneys are very persuasive. Stand up for yourself.

23. Accept responsibility for the outcomes of your work (good or bad). One important part of success is responsibility. When you accept responsibility for your actions, and move forward from there you will feel empowered to make changes. I recommend you ask your clients for feedback on how satisfied they are and work towards continuous improvement.

Those LNCs who cannot accept responsibility will never fully understand why their businesses languish.

24. Monitor the path of your life. Take some time to evaluate your life. Consider where you have come from and where you are likely to end up. Decide whether you want to deviate from this path to achieve a better outcome. And then implement this plan. I recommend doing this for both your personal life and your business. Now is an appropriate time to take stock.

25. Try to strengthen your resolve. The strength of your resolve will determine whether you break down at the sight of a challenge, or whether you dare the challenge to cross your path. You will encounter many success-driven attorneys who pose challenges. They will strengthen your resolve.

Learn from each challenge. In some cases, what you will learn is why you need to avoid working with certain attorneys, such as the one who asked me about my expert's rate. In other cases, you will learn how you need to modify your business. Success is likely to follow.

26. Recognize that there is a lot of competition in the legal nurse consulting field. What can you do to set yourself apart? What is your competitive advantage? How can you stand out in a crowded field? Determine your strengths and weaknesses and develop a plan for building on your strengths and compensating for your weaknesses. I used to think the answer was in correcting your weaknesses. I recall my husband's boss, who said with a straight face that he was going to tackle one weakness a year and within 10 years, he would be perfect. This former CEO narrowly escaped being imprisoned for mail fraud. Could dishonesty have been one of his weaknesses?

27. Dispose of unhealthy habits in your personal relationships. We all have bad habits in our personal relationships. Perhaps we don't listen very well. Or maybe we are very quick to judge. (Legal nurse consulting trains you to be very judgmental.) Don't let these unhealthy habits set the tone for every relationship you have. Instead, extinguish these habits and improve your relationships.

28. Break out of your comfort zone and try new things. Trying new things keeps you thinking and helps you to problem solve. So, make an effort to step out of your comfort zone, experience the world, and learn more.

I recommend continually learning new tips and techniques. Read business books. Listen to podcasts such as Legal Nurse Podcast at podcast.legalnursebusiness.com. Stretch your mind.

29. Try to do good things each day. Each day, try to do something good for other people. Leave others better off because of you. Contribute to a charity. Help your spouse with something he or she is dreading.

This should be easy for us as nurses. We have been trained to help others. Whatever you do, try to do something that not only helps someone else, but makes you feel better, too.

30. Strive for transparency in your relationships with clients. Don't hide information. Don't tell the attorney only what he or she wants to hear and not advise the attorney of the weak parts of a claim. This is a sure recipe for the attorney developing mistrust. And, most of all, try to be honest and forthcoming in all your activities.

31. Find ways to put yourself at peace with the world and your life. Give yourself time to relax, read a book, watch a movie or take a walk.

Forgive yourself for the mistakes you have made. Let go of guilt and recognize that time travels only one way. You cannot do anything about the past except learn from it.

Running a successful independent legal nurse consulting practice is a challenge. I work with LNCs who are committed to building their businesses. Let's talk to see if this is the right step for you.

Starting and running a successful LNC business is hard and not for everyone. Be prepared to sacrifice, to work long hours and to continuously learn. Entrepreneurship gets into your blood as you begin to experience the joys of being your own boss.

CHAPTER 2

Why Small Businesses Fail – And What You Can Do So Yours Won't

You've probably heard that many small businesses fail, right? Are you worried that yours will be one?

Discover Card conducted an independent survey to shed light on the characteristics of the 22 million small business owners in the United States. The number one motivation of entrepreneurs was independence. Most small business owners would not give up the freedom that comes along with owning their business. They do not want to work for someone else, even if it meant making more money.

Successful Legal Nurse Consultants are Unemployable

Successful legal nurse consultants are unemployable. What does that mean? My husband, who has been self-employed since 1980 and I often comment that we could not get jobs now if we wanted to. We think like entrepreneurs.

How Entrepreneurs Think

- "I shouldn't have to wait for approval of anyone to make a change in my business. I can make it today and have it in place immediately."

- "Bureaucracy drives me nuts."

- "I could tell her how she could run her businesses more effectively and efficiently."

- "I can't stand to sit in boring, pointless meetings. Look at all the work I could be getting done."

- "I value myself too much to lower my standards and do something dishonest."

- "Political games are useless."

Why is it Better to Work for Yourself Than Someone Else?

1. You will always make a higher income in a successful business than you will if you are an employee – unless you are working in a very unusual situation as an LNC. When you are an employee you are dependent on someone else's concept of your worth – who will pay you accordingly.

2. As an employee, you will not have freedom to take risks that affect their company. You will need to ask permission to do what you think is best for the company.

3. You will always be bound by someone else's rules if you are an employee. Rules have a purpose - to prevent confusion and give structure. In your own business you make your own rules.

4. As an entrepreneur, you will work harder to ensure your own success than you will someone else's success. I remember a conversation I overheard when I had a policy that unused sick days disappeared at the end of the year. One of my employees told another one, "You might as well call in sick. You are entitled to the day and you lose it if you don't use it."

What a change the following year, when the policy allowed employees to accumulate sick days! Suddenly they were much healthier and not using sick days unless they were really sick.

Successful legal nurse consultants have the entrepreneurial spirit that sets us apart. Only 5% of the world are entrepreneurs. You are special.

The Risk of Why Small Businesses Fail: Isolation

But there is a danger to being too independent as an entrepreneur. This one trait of extreme independence can be the biggest roadblock to success for entrepreneurs. No one person has all the answers. No one person can work alone, always aware of potential problems or roadblocks. Everyone has their blind spots.

Independent legal nurse consultants must be aware of the need to seek out a trusted network of peers. Entrepreneurs need a place where they can discuss issues with others in a comparable situation. Sometimes, when working alone, it is very easy to continue down the wrong path until suddenly you discover what a costly error you have made.

One of the goals of my mentoring program at LNCAcademy. com is to help LNCs avoid expensive mistakes. Believe me, I've made them, and I guide LNCs so they won't.

Why Should You Learn from Successful Business Owners?

While we are talking about isolation, are you guilty of the tempting trap of associating only with other legal nurse consultants? Or are you seeking out other business owners through the Chamber of Commerce, networking groups and other small business owners?

Some small businesses in your geographic area are thriving. Do you wonder what they are doing different from their competitors to attract and retain clients? What lessons can you apply to marketing to attorneys? Go *outside* the legal nurse consulting industry to get answers. Find smart people in other industries, in other businesses that appear to be successful. Watch how they market, advertise, and interact with their clients.

Find Out What You Can Learn from Successful Business Owners

I challenge you: go find them. Legal nurse consultants don't often think about going outside of our field to meet other people who have similar issues. We talk a lot within our profession, but we don't realize how much we can learn from people who are running their own businesses and dealing with these same issues.

My business changed for the better when I found the National Speakers Association (NSA) through a nurse that I know who is a member. It's probably the biggest thing that I did to open my eyes to a world that exists of supportive people who are speakers — speakers are, in fact, "experts who speak".

My exposure to NSA made me aware of internet marketers and I got on some mailing lists. I formed a mastermind of NSA speakers in 2008 and continue to run that group. I joined a couple of coaching programs which also expanded my concepts. This has made me much more aware of providing useful content and focusing on the needs of the target market. It taught me to ask, "What can I do to help you resolve your issues?"

Great marketing is great marketing – whether you're a legal nurse consultant or a podiatrist or a dentist or a guy running a hair salon. The basic concepts are the same. They're adaptable to any business and they work. Get out of your niche and talk to other small business owners. You will be glad you did.

Working In and Not On your Business

Another challenge that entrepreneurs face was discussed by Michael Gerber in his classic book *The E-Myth Revisited: Why Most New Businesses Fail and What to Do About It.* Gerber talked about the importance of working ON your business and not IN your business.

But how do you change from being a day-to-day business "technician", dealing with attorneys and putting out fires, to spending time as a visionary executive looking at your business from the outside in? The best way: schedule committed time to work "on" your business!

If you are like most entrepreneurs, who have created the "busy business noise" in which it can be difficult to even hear yourself think, you will have to structure your time in such a way that the urgencies of the moment will not deter you from this important work. You and your business will benefit from a structure which ensures that you use the time you allocated for exactly what you intended, regardless of the emergency du jour.

One of the things I do is to set aside every day for learning. I read for an hour a day at night and spend at least 2-3 hours a week learning something new. Then I apply the information in my business.

Small businesses fail because of many factors, and one of them is not keeping up and engaged working on your business.

CHAPTER 3

Top Tips for a Successful Life Care Planning Business

What does it take to run a successful life care planning business? You have mastered the fundamentals of Life Care Planning, and you have gotten some cases, but you know you could be doing more to build your business or improve cash flow. Successful Life Care Planners pay attention to five pillars:

- expertise,
- marketing,
- client management,
- finance, and
- business development.

I call these pillars because they form the foundation of your business. They support you and allow you to grow. These 5 pillars also apply to any self-employed legal nurse consultant.

Expertise is a Foundation of Successful Life Care Planning Business

Attorneys understand that Life Care Planners are usually needed for large damages cases involving a patient whose survival will depend on complex care. There is a lot at stake in such cases including factors that we may not see.

For example, plaintiff attorneys may have taken loans to finance a large case. Defense attorneys are concerned about large settlements or awards and how they might affect their relationship with the carrier. Everyone wants to know, "What are the numbers?" Your expertise affects the answers to that question.

Your Life Care Plan must be well written, well researched and easy to follow. The people who will read your plan are not healthcare providers and thus need adequate explanations and a medical summary written for lay people. Spell out abbreviations and define terms. Use a format with sufficient white space. Be sure your tables are clear and easy to comprehend.

Although an attorney may attempt to apply pressure to influence your calculations, remember your role in being impartial. A Life Care Planner hired by the defense attorney may see items a plaintiff's Life Care Planner missed, items that would improve the quality of the plaintiff's life.

Whenever you prepare a Life Care Plan, envision yourself being cross-examined about why you included specific elements in a plan. Your expertise is founded on your detail-oriented analysis of the patient's needs and is rooted in your up-to-date knowledge of medical and nursing care.

Remember that your work product is of no value if you do not meet the attorney's deadlines. You can destroy your successful Life Care Planning business by gaining a reputation of being undependable.

Learning never stops. You aren't the same person you were a year ago and you will be different a year from now. Keep your eyes open for learning opportunities. How do you demonstrate your expertise? Do you share your knowledge with attorneys in the form of newsletters, ezines, and special reports? These are all ways to pull people to you. Do you demonstrate expertise in your analysis of cases? Do you draw on others with specific expertise to help you handle a case that is beyond your experience? How do you maintain your expertise? Are you continuing to learn key concepts you need to build a business?

Marketing

Just about every Life Care Planner needs to market to start or maintain a business. This is the second pillar of a sound business. "Push" marketing involves reaching out to attorneys through networking, cold calls and cold visits. "Pull" marketing reverses the dynamics by using methods to attract clients. Both types of marketing have a role in building a business (Lockard, 2016).

The goal of any marketing is to establish rapport with the prospect, to help that person know, like and trust you, as well as remember you when a case comes in that needs a Life Care Plan.

Your ideal client

- Who do you want to work with? It is far easier to get cases when you have a clear picture of who needs your services.

- Who is your ideal client?

- What market do you best serve?

- What types of cases are the ones where you have the deepest knowledge?

- How can you get known as the go to Life Care Planner for that type of case?

Both attorneys and legal nurse consultants hire Life Care Planners. They may find out about your services through listservs, networking, word of mouth referrals, your website, publications, or a booth at a trade show.

Legal nurse consultants may hire you as a subcontractor or refer you to an attorney. This is often an ideal arrangement if subcontracting provides you with support such as organized medical records and report proofreading services. Marketing requires persistent, consistent effort.

Consider your referral sources. Who else markets to the attorneys who have cases that require Life Care Plans? Get to know the engineering firms that handle accident investigations. Network with the vocational experts, demonstrative evidence firms, and economists who get involved in cases with medical damages. Request introductions to attorneys who may be able to use your services.

Consider all of the demands on your prospect's attention. How do you stand out? Do you stress the benefits of your services, rather than provide the same tired list of services every other Life Care Planner enumerates? Do you demonstrate you understand the attorney's world and frustrations? Does your website make you stand out? Are your marketing efforts working to build a successful business?

Are you blogging?

Analyze how you stay in touch with clients to remind them of your existence. Do you have a website with a blog? Blogging is a way for an expert witness to demonstrate expertise and get the attention of those who are in hiring positions. After doing the work to formulate a thoughtful, informative blog, don't stop there. Repurpose your blog posts in a newsletter that you send out a minimum of once a month. Provide helpful tips in a form that is quickly digestible.

Ask your own clients for referrals. Give them specific language to use in a phone call or email to a colleague to pave the way for your conversation with the prospect (Newman,

2013). For example, ask your client to say, "Bob, I want to introduce Grace Galley, a Life Care Planner who has been helpful to me in my personal injury cases. I know you handle similar cases and think it would be of value to have a conversation with her. She will be calling you. Please take a moment to talk to her."

Client Management

Maintaining sound relationships with clients is the third pillar of a sound business. It costs five times more to market to a new prospect than it does to retain satisfied clients (Saleh, n.d.). Your reputation and ability to establish strong relationships with attorneys will make or break your business.

In general, attorneys are quick, intelligent, and great negotiators. They are trained to win. They need your help to do so. They like stability. When they find a great Life Care Planner, they prefer to stay with that person. Encourage client loyalty by taking a hard look at how you care for customers.

Everyone is increasingly aware of the power of social media to spread both complaints and compliments about your services. Attorneys are networked in ways that may be invisible to you. They participate on listservs and share recommendations with each other.

Look at each step of your process of handling your clients. What can you do to make them feel even more cared for, respected, and valued (Sandler, 2015)? Do you acknowledge receipt of records? Do you ask for feedback on your Life Care Plan? Do you ask your clients what you should stop doing, start doing, or continue doing? We are often surprised by the answers we get when we ask our clients these questions.

You've heard that 80% of your work comes from 20% of your clients. Who are your best clients? What do you do to make them feel even more special? People love to be appreciated and acknowledged. How often do you connect with them or send them a small gift to show appreciation?

People like people who are personable, relate to them, show interest in them and are flexible when possible. Attorneys respond well to Life Care Planners who are easy to work with, understand them, and are just plain nice people. How do you maintain relationships with your attorney clients? How do you make them feel special? How do you reward the attorneys who give you a lot of work? How do you react when an attorney has a complaint about your services? Do your clients perceive you as fair? Do you get rid of the undesirable clients?

Finance in a Successful Life Care Planning Business

Creation of Life Care Plans can consume dozens of hours of your time; some attorneys are surprised by the size of the invoice. Head off collection problems by following some best practices. First, set the expectations at the beginning of the case regarding the sizes of invoices. Although it is never possible to make precise predictions of how many hours it will take to prepare your plan, you should, with experience, be able to give a range of hours.

Secondly, obtain a retainer. Require at least 10 hours. You can double that amount for most involved Life Care Plans. I also recommend you ask the attorney to replenish the retainer before you exhaust it. Asking for another retainer when you have used 75% of the existing one is a great plan that keeps cash flowing.

A practice of asking for replenishing retainers demands that you keep on top of the total number of hours you have spent on the case and anticipate when you will be depleting the retainer. You have the option of stopping work while waiting for the new retainer. Being proactive in requesting additional money is essential when the client is new or has an uneven payment history.

There are several opportunities in the life of a case when you can use leverage. You have leverage when the attorney needs the report submitted by a certain date or when you are noticed about a deposition or asked to analyze opposing counsel's Life Care Plan or to appear at trial. Use leverage to obtain payment.

If you are not working from retainer to retainer, don't allow large numbers of hours to accumulate without payment. And don't avoid or delay collection efforts. Sometimes it is easy to put off collection efforts in the hopes that the check will appear in the mail or because you are distracted by cases.

Your bills won't wait. The most important financial best practice is to know your profit and loss, your expenses, and your accounts receivable. Know your numbers.

You need to know what to charge, how to charge, how to collect your money and how to avoid being burned by attorneys. Cash flow is the sound underpinning of your business. It does not matter how much attorneys owe you; it matters how much money is in your bank. The ideal is to get into a situation where attorneys owe you very little money and instead you are using retainers to pay yourself. Cash flow will make or break your business. Are you paying adequate attention to your finances? Are you charging a fair amount given your location and your skills? Do you have a sound financial basis for a successful life care planning business?

Business Development

Business development is the last pillar. It encompasses examining your operations and looking for opportunities to add new services or improve your efficiency.

- Are there aspects of your business that pose roadblocks?

- Are there services your clients are asking for that you should add?

- Are you listening to what your clients are saying and open to ways to expand?

Some Life Care Planners grow by adding research assistants, who may be effective in collecting the data you need for the plan, and thus improve your efficiency. Subcontractors expand your capability to respond to new cases.

Although there is a degree of training and supervision needed to work with another person, the rewards are great. Subcontractors enable you to accept the case you might have had to turn away because you were already committed to another case. Without subcontractors, your ability to generate income is limited to the number of hours you can work.

Conclusions About a Successful Life Care Planning Business

The five pillars work together to grow your business. You show your expertise in your work product and use it to attract clients and cases. You manage your clients to satisfy their requirements and generate repeat business. You handle your invoicing and retainer requirements so that you maintain a healthy cash flow. You market your services in an effective way. And you use business practices that enable you to leverage your time and expand your capabilities.

This chapter was originally published in the Journal of Life Care Planning, Summer 2017.

References

Lockard, P. (2016, February 3). Why you need push marketing and pull marketing, [Blog post]. Retrieved from **https://www.dmn3.com/dmn3-blog/why-you-need-push-marketing-and-pull-marketing**

Newman, D. (2013). Do it! Marketing. New York, NY: American Management Association.

Saleh, K. (n.d.). Customer acquisition vs. retention costs – statistics and trends. [Blog post] Retrieved from **http://www.invespcro.com/blog/customer-acquisition-retention/**

Sandler, D. (2015). Nice guys finish first. Melbourne, FL: Motivational Press

CHAPTER 4

Traits of Successful Legal Nurse Consultants

Lots of nurses are aware of legal nurse consulting. Many have taken a course to prepare for this field. *Few are successful.* Here are some traits that lead to being a successful legal nurse consultant.

Five Years of Clinical Experience as an RN

The longer a nurse has been clinically active, the more knowledge and experience the nurse will bring to the evaluation of the attorney's cases. Each year of clinical service results in a vast wealth of knowledge.

Certification in a specialty area of nursing is definitely a plus. Certification validates competency in a specialty area and is independent of the state licensure. The type of clinical experience may vary.

Nurses with experience in orthopaedics, for example, have immense value to add to many personal injury cases. Nurses with labor and delivery expertise may wish to be expert witnesses or work for a firm that focuses on medical malpractice associated with birth injury.

Licensed practical nurses are not considered to have the requisite educational background to provide legal nurse consulting services.

Some Type of Preparation

Routes into the field of legal nurse consulting vary. Nurses learn legal nurse consulting from online courses, webinars, college, multi-day or weekend courses. Before you get out your credit card, carefully consider the total investment in terms of time and money.

Sales Ability

How high is your emotional intelligence? Successful legal nurse consultants must possess some sales skills. You are selling your capabilities to assist attorneys, the value of your services, and the outcomes the attorney will achieve by using your help. Your business will flounder without sales skills. All business people need a degree of sales ability to develop and maintain a business. Differences in style and personality are not central to success.

Optimism

Ever notice that the best sales people tend to look on the bright side? Mitch Anthony, author of *Selling with Emotional Intelligence* says; "Most top sales professionals, who are at the top of every achievement chart, tend to be optimistic." Optimism will also tend to determine how resilient a sales person will be. You must be optimistic that you will succeed in building your LNC business.

Resilience

The ability to be committed to your business is the spinal column of emotional intelligence in sales. It's the ability to take fifteen "no's" before you get a "yes" from an attorney interested in using your services. Remember, every no brings you closer to a yes.

Self-Motivation

Most experts and managers believe this is a trait that cannot be taught. Whether it's being driven by money or recognition or simply pride, the best sales people tend to have an inherent competitive drive. It is this factor that leads you to constantly learn – how to market, how to improve the operations of your business, how to prepare better reports, and how to more efficiently provide your services.

There are many ways for successful legal nurse consultants to learn today - mastermind groups, webinars, coaches, books, online courses, audio CDs and more. Take advantage of the vast amount of information available to legal nurse consultants. If you are not learning, you are stagnating.

Successful LNCs recognize where they have holes in their knowledge and they fill them in. The wonderful thing about learning is that holes keep appearing. And we keep learning how to strengthen our businesses to make them successful.

Person-ability

Being friendly and sociable is a hallmark of successful legal nurse consultants who network well and maintain long-term customer relationships. Quite simply, attorneys need to like you and feel comfortable with you.

Empathy

This trait may underlie all other emotional intelligence skills, because it involves truly understanding the client. It involves being intuitive and perceptive. It also requires superb listening and communication skills. It means being able to put yourself into the shoes of your attorney client and tailoring your approach accordingly.

Start Slowly to be a Successful Legal Nurse Consultant

As your business grows, a common growth pattern is to add secretarial support first, then become affiliated with a partner or nurses who will serve as subcontractors. These subcontractor nurses will ordinarily perform legal nurse consulting services for you on a per project basis. As the business expands, you may add nurses as part-time or full-time employees and will then be responsible for paying salaries, benefits, and taxes for these assistants.

Good Written and Oral Communication Skills

A successful legal nurse consultant is an active listener. Effective communication skills are important when working with the attorney or talking with the various physicians, nurses, scientific or healthcare provider experts, and defendants.

You must be able to teach the attorney scientific and medical information so that the attorney can use it to review, litigate, settle or defend a case. It is imperative that you can put complex, confusing information into words easily understood by the lay person.

You should possess the skills to accurately proofread various documents and be able to amend documents without modifying the specific content.

Organized and Analytical

The ability to take complex information and organize it in a logical fashion is one of the most important skills you bring to the legal arena. Organizational skills assist you when sorting through and organizing medical records, developing case strategies, suggesting which expert witnesses to retain in what order, and managing the volume of paper generated by a lawsuit.

In many cases the records tend to be voluminous and repetitive. You should possess the skills needed to organize this material into a format which makes it easier to review.

Resourceful

You are called upon to ferret out medical information, develop exhibits, and suggest case strategies. A successful legal nurse consultant connects with other LNCs through listservs and professional associations such as American Association of Legal Nurse Consultants, American Association of Nurse Life Care Planners and others.

Easy to Work With

Rarely can nurses choose to not care for a difficult patient. They may develop a plan of care to deal with the angry, manipulative, or withdrawn patient. Attorneys experiencing the pressures of practicing law, taking depositions, or preparing for trial or settlement conferences can experience stress that manifests itself in a variety of ways.

The LNC is often a helpful support person in these circumstances. You must be able to work with a range of personalities, some of whom are challenging, and some who flare under tight deadlines and stress.

Not every nurse has the ability to be an LNC. The special communication skills, detective-like thinking, detail-oriented behavior, and ability to teach and research are not universally present in all nurses.

Strong Research Skills

Strong Internet search skills are a must including those needed for medical literature searches, obtaining hard copies of journal articles and medical text books, locating current contact information for medical providers and doing background checks of defendant physicians and opposing counsel's experts.

Persistence

It takes effort, the ability to deal with rejection, and resourcefulness to launch and sustain an LNC practice. It takes persistence to plow through voluminous medical records, to find the details that are important for a case. It takes skill to manage your office practice, to obtain and satisfy your clients. It is well worth it.

My husband and I often talk about persistence. He gets easily overwhelmed by a big task. I talk to him about the need to break down big tasks into little pieces. This is something we do well as nurses. We get a clinical assignment at our jobs and break it down into pieces by multitasking. Somehow all the treatments, medications and daily care get done.

Practice makes perfect. We've heard that mantra since we were kids. Persistence is the key to master anything. You can practice something once every two months and not get very good at whatever you are doing. On the other hand, persistence will almost always deliver results.

- Unless you have a steady flow of repeat business, you need to keep your focus on marketing. Steadily reaching out to new prospects, participating in networking events, and sharing your expertise brings results.

- Accomplishing a medical record review takes persistence. You need to assemble the material, organize it, read it, synthesize it, analyze it and document your findings. All of this takes focusing, turning off distractions, and being persistent.

- With all the daily distractions, from phone calls, to email, to requests from friends and family, it can be a difficult proposition to keep focused. Putting aside those distractions will free you to become better and to get more done.

- Be persistent in your billing practices. Promptly send out invoices, follow up on overdue invoices, and apply interest as needed.

If you really want something, you will do whatever it takes to make it happen.

CHAPTER 5

The Way Successful LNCs Think

What makes the difference between an LNC who builds a successful business and one who never recovers the investment in time and money for an educational course to become an LNC? It has a lot to do with the way successful LNCs think.

You are in Control of The Results

Success is based on your efforts, persistence, determination, and not on a whim of fate or luck. Sure, there are some successful LNCs who were in the right place at the right time, but the point is that they did not get to that place by accident.

I know an LNC who got her start 20 years ago when she saw an advertisement for a public meeting for victims of a certain diet supplement. She went to the meeting and introduced herself to the attorney to see if he needed help with the cases he had signed up. He did, and she grew her business from that meeting. She deliberately went to the right place at the right time.

Observe What Other Successful LNCs Do

Do you associate with successful people or with people who whine? I listened to CDs many years ago recorded by Tony Robbins. He talked about his deliberate plan to study what successful people did and to mimic that behavior.

Whiners will sap your energy and divert you from your goals. Successful people are positive and will encourage you. Draw your strength from them.

Making Money is Essential for Success

You are not a charity; you are not a bank for your clients. You may choose to do an occasional favor for a client and not charge, but you should not let pro bono work swamp your for-fee work. Remember this statement: *Businesses fail because of lack of cash flow.*

If you are having trouble collecting on your invoices, look at what you need to do differently. Are you billing for your learning curve? Are you collecting a large enough retainer to complete each phase of the work? Are you ignoring warning signs that you are going to have a collection issue? (This is a broad generalization: warning signs include solo practitioners, clients new to you and any attorney who tells you what a rotten job another LNC did and how he did not pay her.)

Stick to Your Guns When It Comes to Fees

An attorney protested having to pay for travel time. One of my experts needed to drive 4 hours to attend a trial. We quoted a fee based on the travel time, preparation time and time spent in court. My response to the attorney was, "Unless you can figure out a way to teleport her to the courthouse without her having to drive, there is no way to reduce the fee."

Years ago, I talked to a physical therapist expert witness. He said, "I tell the client, 'My fee is my fee is my fee.'" Don't let your client set your fees.

Let me be clear: Do you have to be flexible now and then? Yes, but any concession should be rarely given and if you do, make sure the client realizes the enormous favor you have done.

You have Precious Resources to Sell – Time and Expertise

Guard them from interruptions, distractions, pro bono plaintiffs calling you with their sad stories, and other time wasters.

Successful LNCs Create Weekly and Monthly Goals

Use a Word file or Excel document to keep track of them. Everything you do should be consistent with your goals. Delegate to others those activities that are not consistent with your goals.

Part 2:

Your Business

CHAPTER 6

Are You Working on Your Busyness or Your Business?

Mastering productivity and time management is critical to running your business well. Too often, though, business owners sacrifice their physical, spiritual, or emotional health. Without these elements, it's difficult to run a robust and satisfying business.

The Obvious and Hidden Benefits of Productivity

Legal nurse consultants and life care planners are interested in getting more done. What are the obvious and hidden benefits of being more productive?

An obvious benefit is that if you focus on the right things, you're going to not only get more done, but also these accomplishments will be the ingredients that make a difference. The hidden benefit of productivity is that you can use the time saved to practice healthy behaviors and put more time into social relationships.

If you are juggling the demands of a part time business on top of a full-time job, or you're managing a family, working full-time, and growing a business, you tend to give less attention to your health and your social relationships. I give you tips about your health in part 3 of this book.

People say things like, "When my business gets to this level, then I'll focus on my health or my relationships." "When I make this amount of money, then I will focus on myself." Increasing productivity benefits you by allowing you to work and save more money and time because you don't waste time doing tasks that aren't going to show a return on investment.

I remember a very busy month earlier this year when I was working days and days on end trying to get ready for a big event. I found myself driving to restaurants for takeout, frequently eating out, and not going grocery shopping. I discovered that I wasn't eating very healthfully because it's hard to get the kind of diet that I follow in restaurants.

Emotional health, physical health, and mental and spiritual health are all foundations for our business productivity.

We also need to consider the effect of un-productive busyness on our health. Stress and overwork may not cause autoimmune diseases or other physical conditions, but a very high-stressed, high-intensity, high-achieving lifestyle can trigger illness. As nurses, we know this, and it's painful to learn the hard way that our lifestyles have compromised our health. Although "an ounce of prevention is worth a pound of cure" is a cliché, I recommend taking it seriously.

Myths about Productivity

We need to understand what true productivity means. We must recognize the difference between being busy, being productive, and being effective. People may feel they can't help being busy, but a closer look will reveal that they've chosen a busy life and work style. A lot of times LNCs work on their busyness rather than on their business.

When we're busy, we're prioritizing everything as important. In that kind of value system, you could pick up paper clips all day and consider this a productive activity. You might pick up a thousand paper clips, but that "productivity" doesn't advance your business or teach you anything at the end of the day.

Identify Busy Work

Think of the value of what you're doing. Is it moving you towards the fulfillment of a goal? Or is it busy work?

People wear "busy" like a badge and become almost martyrs. They reach the point where they're boring because all they talk about is how busy they are. When somebody ceaselessly talks about how busy they are, either they don't prioritize effectively, or they're taking on too many things. Maybe they don't have the skills or the resources to outsource appropriately, or they don't know how to say no or understand what's important to turn down. They need to see the fine line between busy, productive, and effective.

Several years ago, some legal nurse consultants were putting together a book. It was clear to me from their progress that they needed somebody to act as an editor to pull the material together and make it coherent. I realized that just because I had the skills to help them did not mean that I had to volunteer to do it. I saw no clear benefit to myself in doing that. It was an activity that didn't match any of my goals.

Set Priorities

It takes some objective thinking to know the difference between working on being busy and working on your business.

When you're a business owner, all things seem important. You know the pieces that need to be accomplished for your business to flow. They're all like little children crying, "Pay attention to me." For example, when you open your email, you may have in your mind that you're doing this to send a message. Then you see five things that you've got to respond to.

To keep yourself focused on genuine priorities, you can adopt this practice. On the last day of the month, look at the next month and determine your top three priorities. These go on a physical board, in a notebook, or on your computer. Base your choices on the three most important activities you need to do the following month to support your business.

Breaking this down further, on the last working day of the week, determine your top three priorities for the next week, which usually relate to the priorities for the month. At the end of each day, determine your top three tasks for the following day.

With daily goals, you can start with a very clear vision of what you need to accomplish first thing in the morning. You are far less likely to get derailed or to procrastinate by working on things that don't matter.

Consider making a rule that at least one of your top three tasks must be completed before you visit your inbox. The inbox contents usually represent another person's agenda.

What is in your inbox? It may be business. There may be requests, but it is never your top priority. Does it need to be addressed? Absolutely, but it's rarely your top task. Starting on that top task first before you ever go to your inbox can help you to see what's going to move a needle, what's going to generate income, and do something to grow your business.

Once you've accomplished your top three tasks, you can move on to those with less priority, again prioritizing among them. The reason for initially choosing three is that three big goals is usually the maximum you can handle at once. Everything else is secondary.

One way to make these priorities clear is to ask yourself: If you were going on vacation tomorrow, what three things would you have to get done today to go on vacation and feel good about it? The most productive day for people is the day before they go on vacation because they don't waste their time on non-relevant actions.

Also consider what you would do if, instead of working your usual eight- or ten-hour day, an emergency occurred, like needing to take a very ill pet to the vet or having to stay at home with a sick child. Imagine that you only have two hours for work. What do you absolutely have to get done in those two hours? Those are your top tasks and your top priorities.

The Importance of Outsourcing

Some business owners tell me that no one can do the job as well as they can. I've talked to legal nurse consultants who understood that to grow their businesses, they had to rely on subcontractors. However, they fear bringing other people into their business to handle those types of cases because they believe that no one is as good as they are. Therefore, there's no point in outsourcing or subcontracting.

Realize that productivity means focusing on what you do best. That may not be marketing. It may not be doing a MailChimp campaign. It may not even be doing sales calls. You might be good at these things, but if they're

$10-an-hour tasks, you are not wisely using your time by working on them if you normally charge $125 an hour.

Even if you're a perfectionist, you may be able to outsource some tasks that will be done well enough, even if not up to your standards of perfection.

Determining your need for virtual assistants means figuring out what types of tasks to assign, finding the right people, and bringing them onboard. Timing is critical in hiring either a virtual or a real-time assistant. You'll need to devote time to training the new person.

Unfortunately, many business owners wait too long because they feel they don't have enough money to hire someone. Then their business does so well that they're too busy to train their assistants. They may blame the assistant for not doing the tasks correctly, but typically, the problem is that they haven't done the proper training with them or that they expect them to read their mind.

If you think you'll be hiring a virtual assistant in the next six months or so, start recording the steps that you do with an online program like Zoom or some other recording software. Write down each step and put it into a manual. That way, you're doing a little at a time, and you aren't overwhelmed with getting the documentation in place and training the new assistant.

Start that manual and continue it even when you have your assistant. No virtual assistant or employee stays at a job forever, and regular updating ensures that a new employee can more easily step into and manage the job. In addition, because there will now be areas where your employee has complete responsibility, have him or her add details to the manual. Have your employee also add new processes or systems to the manual.

Avoid the Temptation of Bright, Shiny Things

Don't try every new app, program, or recommendation that comes along. Try out a couple, and if they work for you, stick with them. Just because something works for one person doesn't mean it will work for you.

People send me links to new systems or tools every day. "Have you heard about this new app?" they ask. They may say, "I use this project management system." They may be surprised that I haven't heard of it, but there are thousands of new apps that enter the iTunes store every day. A person can't learn them all. Stay focused.

I concentrate on a few that help my business, and I only look for alternatives when something is missing. No tool is going to work unless you use it and change the behaviors around that activity. I look first for tools that can help me automate certain functions, like grocery lists and calendars. I list some specific timesaving suggestions at the end of this chapter.

How to Avoid Workaholism

Sometimes the eternal quest for productivity tips over into workaholism. How do we draw the line against that happening?

If you love what you do, it's hard to put that work away, especially if you work from home, which I do. If you are just starting your business and you need cash, it's even harder, but there is a point of diminishing returns when we work so much that we start to lose our effectiveness.

Decision-making power and willpower are finite. Towards the end of the day or when we are tired, hungry, or in need of a break, we start making status quo or fear-based decisions. We have less creativity and ability to solve problems.

It is extremely important to take breaks, not just throughout the day, but also to have at least one day a week where you don't work at all. For small business owners that might be tough, especially if this is your side hustle, and you're trying to grow this part of your business on top of a full-time job.

I have a colleague who was the primary breadwinner in her household. She had six months of cash available. After that, she was broke. She worked constantly, and at the end of the six months, she was diagnosed with Hashimoto's disease.

Her business coach had been telling her that she had to take off one day a week. She argued that she needed money too badly to do that, but when she looked back at this time span, she realized that she would have been able to take off that day.

Once she adopted the practice of taking a day off every week, she found that she developed a greater love for what she did. By taking Sundays off, she began to look forward to Mondays.

What can you do on your days off? You can do anything that isn't work related. Read books that have nothing to do with your business. If you spend your weekdays reading to upgrade your professional or medical knowledge or the emails that come to your inbox, read fiction on your days off. If you watch instructional videos during the week, watch funny movies on your day off.

Extend this relaxed attitude to include workday breaks. Go for a walk. Do some yoga or chi kung. Develop a movement practice that reinvigorates your body and mind. Walking, for example, increases creativity and can make us more alert. A Stanford University study showed that students who walked were able to give more creative answers on a test even if they walked on a treadmill.

If you're on the phone and don't need to refer to your computer, walk while you talk. The more you integrate physical activity into your day, the less you find yourself relying on the false energy of sugar and caffeine. It's such a healthy thing to do. Walking is good for our body, getting out in the fresh air and exposed to the vitamin D in the sun.

Be clear on your priorities, and nurture your mind, body, and spirit, and your business will grow organically and be a source of enrichment on all levels.

Bonus: Some Specific Timesaving Tools

If you're an Amazon Prime Member, you'll see a section called "Subscribe and Save." You can automatically order any non-perishable items such as coffee, rice, beans, and dry goods. You set the delivery timing based on your average needs. You also have the option to skip a month.

Your deliveries come to your door. You don't have to go to a big box store. You'll also save money because the more you order, the bigger discount you get.

Some people also use a system called Instacard that deliveries perishable foods such as fruits and frozen and refrigerated products. You can organize your shopping list to highlight the things you order regularly.

Although I haven't yet tried the following service, it sounds worth checking out. This is a clothing rental service called "Le Tote." **www.LeTote.com**. You can get a certain amount of clothing per month, wear it, and send it back. This is all automated.

This service will particularly benefit you if you're a professional. Le Tote, upon receiving the returned clothing, launders them, and sends them out to somebody else. It's like having a giant closet for people to choose from. If you get something you'd like to keep, you can buy it at a discounted rate.

The professional woman who told me about this service says she pays around $50 a month and saves a huge amount of money on clothing. She also saves shopping time. She travels a lot, and the service saves her from having to bring dirty clothes home. She ships them back directly from her hotel. Shipping is free.

Consider these tips for handling your busyness so you can focus on your business.

CHAPTER 7

Your Image

In the previous chapter I shared a tip about using a clothing rental service to look polished. Attorneys constantly judge their experts and consultants by the way they look.

A professional image is important for many people, especially for legal nurse consultants and life care planners who work in environments where appearance counts. Trial attorneys are very focused on how an individual comes across to others. This makes it essential for us to pay attention to presenting a professional appearance.

This is especially important when you are making the transition from a clinical environment where you wear scrubs or a uniform. You come home disheveled and rumpled from a very full shift. You must switch over to an entirely different mindset and environment where how you look is critical.

This chapter will help guide you in presenting the most professional image possible.

From Scrubs to Suits

Most legal nurse consultants come out of a clinical environment where we're wearing scrubs if we're in the surgical setting or a uniform in non-surgical areas. The original tradition in nursing was to wear white. In more recent years, the trend has shifted to scrubs or colorful patterned tops and pants.

A professional look in the O. R. is very different from one in a lawyer's office. When legal nurse consultants leave the hospital environment and enter the world of lawyers, they need to revise their professional images.

People are always judging you, and these are snap judgments. One study showed that people made decisions about others within about seven seconds. The most important basis for such decisions, whether the individual is giving a speech or engaging in one-to-one conversation is how you look.

If you're spending time now in court, conferences, or in law offices, it's critical to be sure that your image enhances the impression you give. It must be pleasing to the eye in a non-distracting way. Make sure that people trust and like you. Build up trust with a consistently positive and pleasing image that you display every time.

The people I coach have had some debate about what makes for a professional image when you exhibit at an attorney conference. One of the people in my coaching program (LNCAcademy.com) talked about going to an attorney conference and seeing an exhibitor who was wearing surgical scrubs. Usually when women who exhibit wear a pants suit or a pants skirt or a jacket and skirt. Male LNCs and life care planners usually wear business suits.

Having spent a lot of time in exhibition halls and attorneys' offices, I believe that scrubs belong in the hospital, not in an attorney's conference room or an exhibition hall and certainly not in court. I recommend wearing suits and other professional attire.

Sex Appeal Doesn't Sell Legal Services

Well, it shouldn't. At trade shows I've seen women who are marketing to attorneys and wearing skirts that are extremely short and blouses that are extremely low cut. Since your image should say who you are professionally, these women are giving a misleading impression. A professional appearance helps people to believe what you're saying and selling. It's your calling card. It's how you want people to remember you.

Make sure your blouse is not low-cut. You don't want to give a false or distracting impression. You want to be viewed as a professional and as the subject matter expert. The clothes you wear should support an image of you as credible, efficient, trustworthy, and likeable. You want your clothes to reflect your professional performance.

Sometimes skirts cause problems. When you sit down, make sure your skirt doesn't rise. If its structure makes it do that, wear something else. If you're going to be moving around a lot, especially at a networking events, wear pants.

What you wear at networking events is as important as your business card. You want your clothes to be consistent with who you are and what you represent, just as when you're in the courtroom or at the law office. It can be a bit more relaxed but still polished. When you're networking, make sure your attire represents how you want to be remembered.

Color Sends a Message

Color is very important. When you're wearing the right color, it can send a powerful message and elicit a desired response. I recommend avoiding bright colors like reds and pinks. Choose instead navy, gray, or camel with a white or an ecru shirt underneath. Avoid large prints, lace, or colors that don't express professionalism. Remember that the wrong color can send the wrong message.

I saw an attorney once do something fascinating with a color. He was representing a couple who had a large property with many acres of land. One night their son was driving his friends through a field. One of the boys in the bed of the pickup truck was thrown out, landed on his head, and ended up with significant brain damage.

When the case went to court, I was one of the people who was testifying. The defense attorney wore a brown suit, and he advised his clients, who were the father and mother of the driver of the pickup truck, to dress down in clothes that were almost shabby. He referred to these homeowners as humble farm owners rather than the multi-millionaires that they were.

I was fascinated by the attorney's use of color and language to project an image in that situation. It was done very deliberately and specifically to convey a message.

Experts in the realm of what colors mean to people say that brown makes people think *trustworthy.* A business that has used this to its advantage is UPS. This company wants you to think that you can depend on it, i.e., that it's trustworthy. I believe that this attorney was aware of the association of brown with the quality of trustworthiness. He wore brown because he wanted the people in the courtroom to believe that they could trust what he was telling them.

Color and Style: Not Only for Women

The above anecdote shows that men need to be aware as women about the impressions they give. Here are some more recommendations for men.

Avoid big beards. If you really want one, keep it trimmed. Men also need to pay attention to their nails, keeping them neat and clean. (A lot of women don't need to be told this, but if you neglect nails, this advice is for you, too.) Men also need to make sure that their shoes are in good repair because shabby, rundown shoes do not create a professional impression, and people will look at your shoes while you're speaking.

Generally, black is considered a little harsh as a clothing color. I recommend navy, gray, a dark tan, and brown, depending on what message you want to convey. Choose your ties carefully. Avoid those that have bold prints and select instead a small print or a monotone color.

While not a lot of men wear bracelets or other forms of jewelry, don't wear these at all when you're in a professional setting. Stay simple and very conservative in all your attire.

A simple and effective look is to match the shirt and the tie with the suit. Sometimes the tie is optional.

Conduct Counts

So far, I've focused on clothing and accessories, but many other factors affect the kind of impressions we give. Again, this is especially important for legal nurse consultants and expert witnesses, who are often in situations where everybody in the room is concentrating on them. From the moment they walk into a legal-oriented setting, they have a specific purpose: whether it's to market, to teach, or to testify.

Focus on your body language and your communication. Good posture and being aware of your facial expressions are very important, as well as good eye contact and the tone in your voice.

Another thing that's very important is the speed with which you deliver your message. This is very important when all eyes are on you.

View your business life by seeing everywhere you go as a networking event. You never know when you might run into your next client. Be aware of what you're saying and whom you're saying it to because you don't know who that person knows. Always be at your best behavior at networking events because that's how you want to be remembered. That's your calling card.

The people you meet will have your business card. They're going to see what you do, but they are going to remember who you are, how you carried yourself, and how you looked.

Be Consistent

I've heard some stories, particularly in the professional speaking world, of people who, on the stage, are professional, put together, gracious, and nice. They get off the stage and they're nasty to the stagehands. They're not nice to the meeting planner, and they're arrogant.

Stories spread around about the few people who behave that way because they're not congruent in how they're coming across to people. They're not consistent. It's very bad for their business when word gets out that they're prima donnas.

People react positively to you when you are consistent. Every time they see you, you look good. You're nice. You're smiling. You're in a good mood. Those are the types of things that are all associated with our images.

Here's a very tangible example of that. Recently I went out to dinner with my son and a friend. We were in the restaurant as it was closing. We've been there several times before and one of the guys behind the counter said, "We're closing soon, and we've got some leftover soup. You're always so nice to us when you come in. Would you like to take some soup home with you for free?" We said, "Sure, that would be great." They gave us three big containers of this wonderful-smelling soup just because that's who we were. We were nice to them.

Looking nice is one piece of the picture. So is your behavior. It's how you behave in public. You can have the most put-together image in the world, but if you don't act nice, you ruin any work you put into your physical appearance.

To sum up the message of this chapter: Look good. Be kind.

CHAPTER 8

Procrastination: What is the Cost?

Do you ever procrastinate as a legal nurse consultant? Do you put things off until the very last minute and then get stressed out trying to meet the deadline? Do you tell people you work better under pressure?

You may have told yourself that line so many times that you believe it. But the bottom line is, procrastination is costing you and your legal nurse consulting business BIG time! Procrastination is the little monster that eats away at our resolve.

Emotional Cost of Procrastination

Are you a procrastinator? Stress and worry are a routine thing for procrastinators. Many people get moody and depressed. The project starts to feel larger and larger, and you feel less and less confident in your ability to tackle it. Procrastination eats away at your confidence, slowly but surely. Over time your self-esteem decreases, and you add more worry and stress to your life.

Physical Cost of Procrastination

When people procrastinate, the stress often makes them tired and irritable. They get headaches, backaches, irritable bowel syndrome, ulcers, stomach problems, and other stress-related disorders. The stress caused by procrastination will rear its ugly head somewhere in your body. Eating healthy food and exercising help to deal with the stress, but most procrastinators put off purchasing healthy food and heading to the gym too!

Financial Cost of Procrastination

There is also a financial cost to procrastination. People miss deadlines and turn down work. This is especially devastating when you are self-employed. You don't make enough money to pay the bills. You sink into debt. The debt adds more stress. Many people have the money in the bank but fail to pay their bills on time. They put this task off and then forget. Then they have additional fees for delinquent payments. Enough missed payments, and your credit score is hurt. Your financial future could be at stake!

Relationships Cost of Procrastination

You let down your legal nurse consulting or life care planning clients, friends, and family when you procrastinate. You miss deadlines and turn work and in late. This can be devastating to an attorney's case and may set you up for being sued.

Because you are stressed and near deadline all the time, you work all day and evening, which means you have less time to spend with your friends or family. You miss important family events because you put things off and then need to work, or you are running late and show up when the event is half over. You miss your child's part in the play or the first sonogram, etc. Procrastination takes its toll on not just you – but on everyone in your life.

So even if you think procrastination isn't a big deal, it is! It is destroying your life and the longer you put off doing something about it, the more damage it will do to your business.

5 Steps to End Procrastination and Get It All Done

Do you have a lot on your plate? Do you wonder how you will get it all done? Maybe there is just one thing you hate to do, and it seems so overwhelming. Often, legal nurse consultants procrastinate because the temptation to do what makes us happy right now overrides the knowledge that getting our work done will make us happier in the long term.

Putting it off is not the answer. It just feels like a huge weight on your back. So, how will you get it all done?

I have a few tips that will make any legal nurse consulting or life care plan project, no matter how large, easier to accomplish.

Action Tips to Tackle Procrastination

1. Break down BIG projects or goals. Take a long-term project or huge task and break it down in several short-term projects/action plans. Or maybe your to do list is a mile long. Just break up that extensive list into mini lists. You know you have broken it down enough when it can be completed in a brief period, and it does not contain a lot of different steps. When you can complete a task, and check it off your list, it builds momentum and confidence in your ability to follow through.

2. Prioritize. Go through your list of tasks and determine which has top priority. Prioritize clear down to the lowest priority. Take into consideration your priorities, your client's priorities, and how each task blends with the other tasks. For instance, if it is a task that must be done for other tasks to be completed, that increases the priority.

3. Make a plan. Plan how you will accomplish these tasks. Who will you need to call or meet with? Do you need to enlist the help of others? Are there supplies that need to be ordered before you can move forward on a certain task? Make a plan and include lots of details. This will make task completion easier.

4. Schedule time for each task. Actually, put the time you plan to work on it on your legal nurse consulting calendar. Don't just assume you will find a time or that it will just get done. Block out sections of time for this project. Do you need to block out a complete day or two to get this done, or will it be something you can work on an hour here and two hours later (remember that you already broke the long tasks into shorter time frame tasks)?

5. Take action. You can do all the above and it will look good on paper, but nothing will happen till YOU act and work on the project. Getting started is the hardest part. Do whatever is needed to force yourself to get started. Once you get started, you may find it is much easier to do than anticipated. You won't know that until you give it a try.

No matter how big the legal nurse consulting project, putting it off only makes it feel larger. Breaking it down and following the above steps will make it manageable, and before you know it, the project will be completed successfully.

Your LNC success is based on how well you set and achieve goals. Goal setting should be a natural process for us as nurses. Don't we all know how to write patient outcomes? Haven't we heard of SMART goals?

Yet we flounder when it comes to setting business goals, and we get caught up in the to dos and can lose the big picture.

Writer's Block

So, you say, "Wait a minute, Pat. I don't usually procrastinate, but when I have a report I don't know how to write, I get stalled. What do I do then?"

Do you ever find you need help overcoming writer's block? What does this look like? You need to create a legal nurse consulting report, but you are stuck. How do you begin? Here are 6 tips to overcoming writer's block.

1. Get the basics right

Look at what is holding you back. Are you not sure about

- What the issues are in the case
- Who the attorney is representing
- The deadline

Get clarity from your client. You can't do a wonderful job without understanding the framework of your work product. Be sure you identify the issues foremost in the attorney's mind, knowing you may uncover previously hidden issues as well.

Know who hired you. This sounds simple, but I once received an expert report written by one of the experts subcontracting for our company. She wrote a beautiful report – if she was a defense expert. Unfortunately, she had been hired by the plaintiff's attorney.

Thank goodness, we caught it when proofreading the report before it went to the attorney. Because of this experience, we immediately took steps in our letters and emails to experts to reinforce who our client was.

Be clear on when your work product is needed. Don't allow procrastination to keep you from starting the report way too close to the deadline for everyone's comfort. I call this "brinkmanship".

Brinkmanship is the art or practice of pursuing a dangerous policy to the limits of safety before stopping, typically in politics.

2. Overcoming writer's block means checking your mindset

Are you inexperienced and afraid of bungling the work product? Do you believe that if you spent just a little more time (and a little more time which becomes a lot of time) that you could get the report perfect? Are you worried you will spend too much time or get distracted by side issues?

Remember that your mindset can be your worst enemy. Believe in yourself. You have nursing background that gives you great insight into medical issues and makes you valuable as a legal nurse consultant. You probably know more about medicine and how the healthcare system functions than does your client.

The only way you get experience is by doing reports. And keep in mind that perfectionism can paralyze you to the point that you can't start a report for fear it won't be perfect.

3. Disconnect from your distractions

Turn off email. Don't surf the internet. Unplug or mute your phone. (I share more tips about technology distraction in the next chapter.) **Have someone in charge of your children**, if you have young kids, or work after they go to bed. Don't sabotage your work time by allowing distractions to pull you away from what you are writing. If you must check email, set a timer so that you resume working after a 5-minute break.

4. Write first, and then edit

I recommend making an outline of the points you want to cover in your report. It will help the flow and enable you to make sure you are covering the topic. Don't get stuck by a section of your report, or the need to find the perfect phrase. You will find your word flow will improve as you write.

You will always have the opportunity to go back and edit or fine tune your report – that is, if you don't wait until the last minute to write it.

5. Copy and paste from other reports

Do you have certain types of reports that you create over and over? Let's say you are a long-term care expert who commonly cites the Federal regulations that govern nursing home care. Save those sections as files and copy and paste them into an expert report.

If you commonly define certain medical terms, set up a vocabulary file and keep adding to it. I saved files that explain the Glasgow Coma Score, stages of pressure sores, muscle strength testing, pain assessment tools, and many other explanations I typically inserted into my reports.

Be very careful, however, that you do not copy and paste case specific material. I proofread a report for an expert who had used sections of another report she had written – but did not delete the other patient's name and identifying information.

6. Stick to your deadline

Set and stick to a deadline. Put it in your calendar. Know that the sooner you get the report done, the sooner you get to pay yourself for your work (by being able to use the retainer you received). Stay focused and you will have no difficulty overcoming writer's block.

CHAPTER 9

Destructive Technology Addiction: How Does It Affect LNCs?

Most of you are familiar with the destructive nature of alcoholism, drug addiction, and eating addictions. We all, however, need to be aware of an addiction that is rapidly gaining force in today's technological society. This is technology addiction. It can derail your productivity.

Technology addiction is not recognized in the DSM-5, a manual used to diagnose psychiatric issues. However, its symptoms parallel all the criteria for addiction. In simple terms, this means that very often individuals are using technology the same way that drugs or alcohol have been used for years.

Hooked on the Machine

For some people technology is a portal to an alternative reality. When they have nothing to do, many young people turn to their technology. They're primarily communicating through their technology, so they don't have face-to-face interaction. We're seeing it causing problems for individuals around the world.

I remember a family I saw in a restaurant. It consisted of parents and two adorable kids. The father sat there the entire time looking at his phone sending messages and writing emails.

I was positioned so that I could see the mother's face. She would glance up at him with a wistful look that said, "Why are you doing this? Why not pay attention to your meal and us?" But she never said a word. She just sat there, stared at him, stared at the kids, and stared at the phone.

This is an example of technological addiction. More and more studies are coming out showing that this is becoming problematic both for adults and for young people. We're finding many students who basically complain that they can't get their parents' attention because their parents are on their devices all the time. There have been several injuries, abuse cases, and neglect cases where parents have been paying attention to the technology rather than to the children.

Virtual Relationships Don't Develop Social Skills

In many instances, we're seeing and hearing from diverse sources that individuals are not developing the social cues or the social awareness they need because they aren't engaging in direct, face-to-face communication. As a result, they're losing the ability to read facial cues and body language. They seem to behave inappropriately in some settings.

Businesses managers report they're having a very difficult time hiring young people out of college who can think creatively and who can stay with a problem for an extended period because they don't have the frustration tolerance. Also, these young people frequently have a tough time working in groups because they're used to working virtually. When they come into a meeting and must interact with people, read what's going on with them, and communicate effectively on a face-to-face basis, they have difficulty.

Distractibility is another big issue. People are very limited in their ability to pay attention to much of anything. It's very disturbing to notice how much effort some people must make to pay attention for extended periods of time. They haven't developed the skills and the ability to do that.

Also, we're seeing that often people are not taking the time to develop relationships. If you watch young people at bus stops in the morning, they're all on their own devices, and nobody is interacting. The term for that is "Being Alone Together."

In businesses, a lot of times workers rely too much on email and texting. Instead of walking up a couple of cubicles or into the next office to talk to someone with whom they have an issue, they try to resolve the conflict through texting and email. This causes more problems.

You Can't Do Patient Care by Texting

I have great concerns in terms of how young people will engage in health care and helping professions. They're not building the interpersonal skills that they need.

Nursing requires very intimate contact, face-to-face communication skills, problem solving, and critical thinking. We become very aware of this problem as members of the medical malpractice world or the nursing malpractice world when faulty thought processes result in patient harm.

Specialists who work with social workers, teachers, therapists, and nurses share my concern. They report that people in classes can't put their devices away, even during class, to pay attention. Reports have also come out saying that many accidents have occurred because of fixation on electronic devices.

An anesthesiologist in Texas who was looking at his iPad during a procedure was investigated when a patient died on the table. There have been other instances where individuals were not tending to the patient, and the patient fell.

In one case some nurses were looking at wedding photos on an iPad and didn't happen to notice the call bell ringing. The patient fell and received a significant injury, and the nurses were held responsible for that and could have possibly lost their licenses.

The Issues are Complex and Troubling

Some hospitals have blocked the staff's access to Facebook, but that doesn't solve the problem if personnel can access Facebook or other sites using a cell phone or iPad. There have been instances where individuals have taken photos of a hospital setting or even a patient and put that up on a website, causing all kinds of issues—legal, social, and personal.

There are confidentiality issues involving information being sent to the wrong address via fax or email, information being hacked into and possibly even something as simple as hitting the "Reply All Button" when a message should only go to one person.

Confidentiality

I know of a case in Virginia in which a man turned on his cell phone so that it was recording his colonoscopy. It was on the stretcher below the mattress. He wanted to make sure that he didn't miss any of the post-op instructions. He recorded an hour and a half of some very disparaging comments made about him that he listened to when the procedure was over.

He sued the nurse anesthetist, and he got a half-million-dollar verdict for his psychological damages, the humiliation that he felt when he heard what was said about his unconscious body.

In legal proceedings it would not be uncommon for someone to sit in the courtroom and have a recorder in their pocket and be recording the procedures. You can record today with a phone and a pen.

Boundaries

Anyone can walk into a restroom and overhear a very personal conversation, but it's gotten to the point that there's no place where boundaries exist around our technology.

Another problem is that as individuals are texting or tweeting, very often they're sending out extremely personal information with the idea that only the person they're sending it to is going to get it. That person can pass that information on. It can go onto a larger network.

I remember a report of a nurse who was in a hospital setting and tweeted about how bored she was and wished that something would happen with a patient because that would at least give her something to do.

Every system and every organization has its gallows humor. Those are the types of things that you understand because you're part of the organization, but once it gets out, the context totally changes. People can be offended. They can be hurt. They can be bullied.

In this case, people viewed the tweet as reflecting a callous attitude and approach. People may think these things, but when you put it in writing, it becomes very real for everybody.

Overall, we have lots of possibilities of HIPAA violations of confidentiality issues. This is something that LNCs need to be following.

Technology and Reckless Endangerment

I also hear a lot about personal injury cases that occur because a person is distracted, like distracted driving for example.

My son called me once after witnessing an accident. Only because he was particularly attentive was he able to slow down in time to avoid being part of the chain reaction. The police who came to interview him told him that the woman who drove through a stop sign and onto a two-lane road where she hit a car was on her cell phone.

Texting and driving and texting and walking constantly distract people. One of the major problems in major cities today is pedestrians walking out into the traffic oblivious to the cars. One of my colleagues almost hit a woman in Philadelphia because it was raining. He was trying to watch the street signs, the lights, and the other cars. This woman was on her phone and just walked right out into the intersection. If he had not been paying attention, he would have hit her. She never looked up. She was totally focused on the phone.

A friend told me about an experience he had while driving to work. Not too far from his home he saw a young man in the lane across from him, standing in the middle of the road on the white line with his phone in his hand, looking at something. My friend thought, "This man is going to get killed."

The Hypnotic Nature of Technology

I know how easily it is to slip into the habit of checking email like every hour, and then suddenly you're sliding down a rabbit hole. You want to read a link or watch a video and before you know it, time slips by.

Studies have shown that technology is so mesmerizing that it sedates someone prior to a procedure with almost as much effectiveness as some sedative drugs.

The opposite is also true. Some college studies were done in which students went tech-free from Friday night until Sunday night. By Saturday night some of the students were showing up in the infirmary with stress-related ailments.

It reminds me of withdrawal from drugs. How long does it take if you've withdrawn from morphine or heroin before you start going into withdrawal? When people speak of the symptoms they feel when they can't have their phones, it sounds like what counselors hear in detox.

Those in drug withdrawal feel shaky. They can't concentrate. Their attention is on how to get out of the situation and start using again. Their hearts are racing.

Technology-deprived people say the same things. People tell me that if they leave their cell phones at home, it's like having a body part missing. This is an addictive connection.

It's Even More Dangerous Than You Think

I heard some trial lawyers in New Jersey talk about a case involving a man who received tweets from his girlfriend while he was driving a truck. The question was whether the girlfriend was liable for the incident that led to this man tweeting while he was driving. He ran over a couple on a motorcycle, both of whom ended up with amputated limbs. The case went through the court system in New Jersey, and ultimately the higher courts did not accept that the girlfriend was liable.

One very surprising piece of information that I learned was that the hands-free method of driving and talking is not any safer than holding the phone up to your ear. It's not where the phone is, it's the distraction and the loss of attention when you're driving that results in injury.

There are even some studies that show that if the rear speakers in your car are louder than the front speakers, you don't have a balanced perception of the noise. You can increase the potential of an accident by a significant amount because your brain must decide whether to pay attention forward or to pay attention to the sound behind you.

It's true that you can be distracted by eating a hamburger in your car or having a cup of coffee spill in your lap. However, though many things can potentially be distracting, the interactive aspect of technology is becoming so compulsive for some individuals that they just can't stop.

A colleague who was teaching a class about technology addiction was approached by a student who had previously attended one of his classes. The colleague had advised students to put their cell phones in the trunks of their cars.

The former student said, "I really tried putting my phone in the trunk of my car before I went out driving because I feel so compulsive about the need to answer it. I must answer the phone every time it rings."

One core issue is that of being ramped up all the time. If you're on 24 hours a day, seven days a week, what does that do to your nervous system?

From a health perspective, there's no downtime for us. Individuals need to be able to step back periodically to take a breath, to just slow down, and get some control over what they're paying attention to.

Recovery Techniques

Does any of this sound like people you know - or you? Today there are a variety of tools and methods to try to bring people out of that. One method addresses the issue that people spend so much time on their devices that they're not even going to sleep at night, which contributes to their distractibility during the day.

Some experts suggest that people get off all their devices well before bed time. Television is somewhat different because it's across the room, and it doesn't have the same effect. If you're on your phone or on your computer, get off your phone about an hour to an hour and a half before bed because that bright light in your eyes can delay the release of certain chemicals in the brain that trigger your sleep cycles.

Secondly, you tend to get your nervous system ramped up because of your interaction with the device that you're on, so that same time frame of an hour or an hour and a half gives your brain a chance to trigger the chemicals it needs to get you calm.

You can also establish boundaries. Figure out times when you're not going to be on your devices. When you're on vacation, for instance, determine specific times when you're going to check your email (and it's not every hour) like two, three, or four times a day. Again, depending on your job, with the understanding that some people are on call, set some parameters so that you can check email a maximum of four times a day. You will know exactly when you're going to reply and build in some time to do that.

Develop Mindfulness Practices

A researcher at the University of Miami, Amishi Jha, talks about the idea of taking a flashlight in a dark room and just flashing it all over. She makes the point that this is how our attention works today. She talks about the idea that through meditation we can begin to learn to focus that flashlight where we decide to point it rather than just having it control us.

A Question of Balance

- We need to spend time talking to other people face-to-face.

- We need to spend time interacting with family and friends without having the technology continually interrupt our conversations.

- We need to learn to pay attention and do other things that can be relaxing, focusing and getting ourselves to a place where we can interact in a more effective way.

I'm not anti-technology. I use it at work, but when I'm having a conversation with a friend or family member, I know that I don't want the distraction of something buzzing in my pocket. I want the person in front of me to be the most important person at that moment. I've got to pay attention to them. We must be able to control ourselves enough to be able to do that.

The silence mode, the vibrate mode, or the on/off switch can be our friend in that situation. Too many people don't even think about the idea that they have a voice messaging system within their phone that can take messages. They don't have to answer it every time it rings.

LNCs, Be Aware

The technology addiction epidemic affects us as legal nurse consultants on more than one level.

We need to understand the role that technology distraction plays in medical malpractice and personal injury cases and look for evidence of its effects in cases.

We also need to honestly examine the ways in which technology distraction may interfere with our own job performance. Do we turn off the buzzer when we're speaking with a client or interviewing a patient? Do we stop reading medical records to check our messages?

I've made a vow to make sure that I limit the amount of time that I've got that phone on. The more of us who do the same and speak to others about this, the more impact we can have on stemming the tide.

CHAPTER 10

Organizing for Success

As legal nurse consultants and life care planners, our lives are filled with details: cases in distinct stages of progress, various levels of marketing, recent technologies to learn, and many other aspects of our busy days. Consider the impact on you when you can't find a document you need because it's buried beneath a pile of papers or when your calendar has somehow become cluttered with secondary activities. Don't you have more difficulty in smoothly and efficiently running your business? That's why mastering decluttering of both the physical and time-based aspects of our lives is essential.

The Decluttering Conflict

Further on, I'll talk about decluttering your office, but you can lose just as much time that could be spent at work when you must deal with home clutter. Sometimes trying to declutter involves negotiation with a spouse or children. People can feel very differently about the same object.

For example, my husband loves to save things. At times, when I threw things out, he would follow me down to the curb and take them out of the garbage can and bring them back into the house. He is truly oblivious to his environment until it gets out of control.

The only reason we have a modicum of neatness in our house is because of me. If left to himself, everything would be all over. He doesn't even see something as being out of place. It's important to know how to deal with someone who doesn't see clutter as a problem.

Sometimes you need to compromise. Sometimes you must give up on ever retraining a stubborn spouse and stick to decluttering your own possessions. You will see if setting an example persuades a partner or anyone else living in your home to follow suit.

If that doesn't work, keep as much of the house decluttered as possible and assign one or two rooms the other person can keep in whatever state of disorder he or she wants. Ideally this space is a garage or a shed. This is probably the most effective form of compromise.

One Popular Approach to Decluttering

Marie Kondo, author of *The Magic of Tidying Up* and *The Spark Joy Revolution*, recommends that people ask themselves whether each item that they bring into their homes is going to spark joy.

In her method, instead of doing things a little at a time and not feeling like you're getting results, you take a radical approach of sorting things all at once by category. You would, for example, take out all your clothes and put them on the bed or the floor. You then would take each piece of item, hold it in your hands, and ask if it sparks joy.

The physical contact generates a tactile rather than an intellectual response. You could hold it in your hands, see and feel it, and decide if it was something worth keeping. Ask, "Does it energize me?" This approach adds soul and playfulness to what might otherwise be an intimidating or boring process.

The Home Office

When you're starting your legal nurse consulting business, you may find that for several years you'll be running it out of your home in a spare bedroom, in a corner of the living room, or in a den. My first desk was a board placed over the top of two 2-drawer filing cabinets.

When you have a home office, you can't get away from a cluttered or uncleaned house. You may take a short break, go to the kitchen to fix a cup of tea, and see a pile of unwashed dishes. You may walk through the living room and see piles of stacked books that don't fit on the shelves. Messy spaces distract you from the business at hand. They make it hard to focus on what really matters.

These distractions can also inhibit feelings of freeness and creativity. Visual cues that say it's time to vacuum may distract you from reading a medical report. Your space doesn't have to be perfect, but it shouldn't be providing such a huge distraction that you can't focus on the task at hand.

Separating Home and Work

Sometimes people don't make enough of a distinction between work and life. If you want to get serious about your business, you must treat it like a business. If I'm not going to treat myself like a genuine business owner and at least create the place to set myself up for success, then how is anyone else going to treat my business and me with respect?

Consider what your goals are in business. Create a home office space to help you achieve your goals. Keep that space clear and clutter-free.

How I Discovered What I Didn't Need

When my husband and I decided we were going to sell our house in New Jersey and move to Florida, we cleared out our basement. I think I made at least six trips to the Goodwill with bags and boxes full of things. Another person who was helping us made several more trips.

We then changed our minds and decided to keep both the house in New Jersey and in Florida. I have not missed a single thing that we took to Goodwill, and we're living half the year in New Jersey. All that stuff was just extraneous. We weren't using it. It was accumulating in the basement.

The more space you have, the more you fill the space. If you don't have that space, you learn how to keep things compact or make decisions about whether that item really needs to come into your house. If you don't have space for it, you can't accommodate it.

Also, be aware that when you accumulate more stuff, it takes energy to maintain and clean it. Think knick-knacks.

One of the most interesting side effects of physically de-cluttering is that people start to lose weight when they get rid of things. This may suggest that being over-burdened with stuff creates a depression that leads people to eat excessively. With less clutter, they feel more uplifted.

Their health may also improve. Things that have been stored for years accumulate dust. A leaky attic ceiling might contribute to mold on stored objects. Thus, decluttering improves your life on many levels.

Also consider what you may have in storage units. While they may be out of sight and therefore out of mind, keeping space for things for which you don't have room is a very expensive luxury.

Make Finding Things Easy

I know the feeling that my husband goes through trying to find something and how he then starts to berate himself.

He says, "I need to clean up my act" and "I need to get organized."

There's a lot of negative feeling and self-blame that gets generated in trying to find something. This takes away from your positive pursuit of goals, and not being able to find things also means a literal loss of time from your business. Would you rather be marketing or looking for a missing paper? You must stay organized so that you're not wasting time.

Always remember that in working with attorneys we are working on billable hours. We can't charge the attorney for the 15 minutes we spent trying to find the file on the computer we should have placed in a better spot.

Studies have been done showing that people waste 10 minutes a day when they are looking for misplaced items. That's about 3,680 hours or 153 days in a lifetime, so that's a lot of lost productive time.

In addition to clearing out clutter, have fixed places for each of the items that you're often going to use, such as keys, cell phones, and documents. If you have paper documents, make sure they're organized in definite locations. That way you don't have to have six or seven places where your papers might be.

Resist Impulse Buying

Be wary of the temptation to hoard. For example, you might be at Target and see a "Buy Two, Get One Free" deal. You can come home with a lot of things you don't need if you engage in impulse shopping for bargains. If the item is something that you really need within the next week or so, get it. Otherwise, stick to the shopping list.

I do make one exception to this rule. My church encourages its members to take advantage of these deals and gives the items to a local food bank. You can really make a difference in other people's lives by providing those exceptional deals, and they don't have to end up on your shelf in your kitchen—which is really the point of not hoarding.

Decluttering Time

In terms of time clutter, be clear on what's important to you in any area of life. That way you can focus on the items, the people, or the activities that are more pertinent, whether you're working on a health, work, or career goal.

We like to connect with other people. We like to make other people happy, but at the same time we must think about what's important about our goals. If you know what's important, you will focus more on that. That way, when someone is pressuring you, for example, to come to a party or join a committee, your priorities are well defined, and you can decline with a clear conscience.

An approach that addresses both the physical and the time elements of clutter is the mindset of having less stuff and more experiences. Time is our most critical asset. I think most of us value time spent with friends and family more than shopping. If you need activities to get yourself out of the house, consider going to a cooking class or on a trip. Also think about some of the activities you want to do and try to bring them into your calendar, as opposed to mindless consumption.

Decluttering and Productivity

Legal nurse consultants must juggle the demands on their time from family, often from a clinical job, and all the time needed to fit in marketing, networking, and working on cases. One way to declutter your time is to create a sample or model week for yourself.

The core basis for this is the question that life coaches often ask clients who don't know what to do with their lives. The coach asks, "What will happen in an ideal day for you to make it seem like it's a success?" Charting out an ideal week expands this concept.

You could give each day a theme. Monday might be for marketing, Tuesday for case work, and so on. Another way to do this might be to break down each day into units. You might devote mornings to marketing calls or social media work and afternoons to working on cases.

Obviously, you need some flexibility in this scenario. If an attorney wants to see you on Monday morning, you can't make your marketing calls. If you need to be in court on Wednesday afternoon to testify as an expert witness, you not only have to put aside other case work, but you'll need to prepare for court. Nonetheless, having a structure that can accommodate exceptions organizes your time much better than random chaos.

You may want to use an Excel spreadsheet and develop a color code for various activities so that you can see at a glance what you'll be doing. It will also show you where your free time is. A third advantage is that it can show you how to combine tasks, especially those that take you out of the house.

The son of a colleague of mine has a regular tennis practice. She takes him there, and because Wi-Fi is available at the court, she brings her laptop and does some work while he's practicing.

The alternative to time blocking, which we've all experienced, is to have an unplanned day in which we bounce from one thing to another, doing things piecemeal, and ending up feeling drained and disjointed. This can wreck our drive and creativity.

Spend Time to Save Time

Although I mentioned earlier in this chapter that the de-cluttering specialist Marie Kondo recommends a radical assault on clutter, you might feel overwhelmed about taking it on all at once. However, even if you make a commitment to do a little a day, i.e., "Today, I will look at my winter clothes," or "By the end of the week, I will fill a bag for a charity shop," you will make inroads.

The same is true of time clutter. Say, "I will subtract one secondary activity from my schedule this week" or "I will ask myself if this or that activity really benefits me."

This approach may not provide dramatic and instant results, but it will make a difference. It will make your life easier and help your business to grow.

PART 3:

Your Motivation

CHAPTER 11

What is Your LNC Attitude for Success?

Is becoming perfect possible? "Joe" (name changed) on the surface had everything going for him. He was a graduate of an Ivy League college and ran a successful business. He was personable and friendly and made others feel important and respected. But Joe had a piece missing from his personality: a conscience. He was a charming sociopath.

Joe took chances. He was married with two children and a mistress. He asked the person who did his income tax if he could write off as tax deductible the expenses associated with his mistress. (No.) His wife, who was oblivious to the fact of the mistress, loudly declared to me at a party that they had been married for so many years that she was not worried about his faithfulness. Shortly afterwards, Joe left his wife and married his mistress, who was quite wealthy because of having previously married two very successful men.

Becoming Perfect

Joe wanted to improve himself. One time he declared that every year he would correct one character flaw. "At the end of 10 years," he said, "I'll be perfect." Within that 10-year period, he was removed from the CEO position, given a healthy severance check, and somehow rather quickly spent that money. I lost track of Joe for a while until I heard he was arrested.

Avoiding Prison

Joe had come up with what he thought was a brilliant scheme. He advertised a weekend getaway property in another state and collected the rent (through the mail). The people who sent him money drove to the location, only to find a vacant field. After a year of perpetuating this fraud, Joe found out someone had complained and notified the law enforcement authorities. They were waiting for him in the post office when he went to collect more rent.

Mail fraud usually results in imprisonment. How would this Ivy League graduate, former CEO who used to make hundreds of thousands of dollars a year, fare in prison?

Joe avoided going to prison through a combination of luck and negotiation skills, with his defense paid for by his alma mater. He had to make restitution to the people he had defrauded.

Joe went out fighting. Literally. Recently I found his obituary. He died at age 77. I also found a court document. Two years before he died, he was arrested for "defiant trespass, disorderly conduct engaged in fighting, and making unreasonable noise." He was released on a $10,000 bail. His obituary made no mention of his arrests for mail fraud or fighting but spoke in glowing terms of his involvement in his local church. His first wife and their three children were mentioned. His second wife (the mistress) was not mentioned at all, as if she never existed. (He was married to her during the mail fraud years.) The obituary suggested that donations in his honor could be made to his Ivy League school, the one that paid his defense fees for the mail fraud criminal charges.

I did not donate.

What did I learn from Joe's misadventure? Being honest and ethical is essential for being in business. And being perfect is impossible.

Attitude is Everything

Kayla is known as an LNC with an attitude for success. Her clients love to call her because she is always cheerful. She smiles when she talks to them. No request is too difficult for her. She gets tons of repeat business.

Janelle is not so upbeat. She has tried for 6 months to find attorneys who will hire her. No one returns her calls. She feels like her dream of being an LNC is slipping away. When people ask her about her business, she looks down and says, "It's not going so well. I don't think I will ever get a client. I thought this would be easy."

Starting and running a business is hard. It is not right for everyone; don't believe an educator who tells you that anyone can become a legal nurse consultant. You need skills in areas I've called the 5 pillars: expertise, client management, business development, marketing, and finance. (I described these in chapter 3.)

The good news is that you can develop these skills if you have a solid foundation built on being analytical and having writing skills. And you need an LNC attitude for success.

The Importance of Self-Improvement

All of us need to take steps for self-improvement (although Joe's plan for becoming perfect backfired and I don't recommend following his path!) None of us enter the field of legal nurse consulting completely ready to take on the challenges.

When does self-improvement become synonymous with success? Where do we start? I've assembled some tips for you.

Remember Janelle? My comments are directed to her or anyone who is discouraged about his or her business success. Stop thinking and feeling as if you're a failure, because you're not. How can others accept you if YOU can't accept YOU?

When people feel so down and low about themselves, help them move up. Don't go down with them. They'll pull you down further, and both of you will end up feeling inferior.

Think of the world as a large room that gives you lessons. You try something; you see if it works. You try something else. Don't feel stupid and doomed forever because your business is slow. There's always a next time. Make room for self-improvement. It takes place one day at a time.

Self-improvement results to inner stability, personality development, and SUCCESS. It comes from self-confidence, self-appreciation, and self-esteem.

Create a Better YOU

Set meaningful and achievable goals. Self-improvement doesn't turn you into the exact replica of the most successful LNC who ever worked in the field. It aims to result to an improved and better YOU.

When you're willing to accept change, and go through the process of self-improvement, it doesn't mean that everyone else is. The world is a place where people of different values and attitude hang out. Sometimes, even if you think you and your LNC friend always like to do the same thing together at the same time, she would most likely decline an invitation for self-improvement.

Remember that there's no such thing as "overnight success." It's always a wonderful feeling to hold on to the things that you already have now, realizing that those are just some of the things you once wished for.

A very nice quote says that, "When the student is ready, the teacher will appear." We are all here to learn our lessons. Our friends, colleagues, business associates and clients... they are our teachers. When we open our doors for self-improvement, we increase our chances to head to the road of success.

Turn a Negative into a Positive

Pain may sometimes be the reason why people change.

- You are discouraged at the slow pace of building your business.
- You've been searching for a better way to handle your invoicing, so you don't struggle to collect from your clients.
- You feel inferior to your competitors.

One of my competitors used to brag about how he took time off to go to vacation in warm places. He would play the one-upmanship game of comparing his vacations with mine. Instead of feeling inferior to him, I thought, "Good. While you are away, attorneys looking for an LNC will call me."

Look for what motivates you in your business. Getting a complaint from an attorney forces us to look at what went wrong. Debts remind us of our need to focus on our business and its stability. It may be a bitter experience, a friend's tragic story, a great movie, or an inspiring book that will help us get up and get just the right amount of motivation we need to improve ourselves.

CHAPTER 12

How to Combat Your Worst Enemy

While everyone has individual worst enemies, everyone has a shared one. It's ourselves and our negative thoughts. This chapter focuses on negativity about aging. It's never too soon to address these feelings directly and to embrace age esteem, the positive attitude towards aging. We need to think differently about ourselves to set our inner selves free to shine, share our talents, and act on our dreams at every age.

Age esteem affects us as legal nurse consultants and life care planners in many ways. Professionally, you may be working with attorneys who are representing elderly people. (Note: your definition of elderly changes as you get older. That's just a warning for those of you who are not quite caught up to where I am.) The value of a case may be based on the age of the person, whether the person was working or not or had dependents. The issue of age and how people age is a part of litigation.

It also affects you personally as a legal nurse consultant. Nurses on average across the United States are in their 50s.

The baby boomer population is moving into the retirement years. This raises questions for everyone in that generation about what they see as their opportunities to contribute and how productive people are and continue to be as they age. I speak to many LNCs who view the profession as a terrific way to transition out of a demanding clinical role.

Finally, you might be caught up in issues regarding elderly parents or siblings where age esteem and aging factors are affecting your interactions.

Age Esteem Equals Self-esteem

Age esteem involves feeling good about yourself at the age you are today, being happy to look in the mirror and realizing that you have a little more character in your face. It also stands for admiration and respect for aging and what it represents.

To do this, we need to honestly face the stereotypes that exist about older adults. One of the perceptions is that older people are slow. We're not too productive. It takes us a while to catch on to what's going on. We take too much of another person's time. We're probably a bit feebler, so why waste good medicine on us? Why not just give us a pink pill and send us home?

Younger people may use expressions like, "Well, hurry, grandpa" or "What's wrong with you, grandma?" These are very unflattering statements.

Recently my husband was speaking to a physician's office. He has received urological care from this doctor. He was calling about an appointment that he has coming up, and the receptionist, who was not particularly bright, was telling him that he needed to obtain his medical records to provide to the urologist.

My husband explained, "I've gotten all of my care in your department in your building, so that all should be in your computer system." She said, "Oh, no, sir that's not possible. You have to find out those results." He kept insisting that it was all in the computer, and she said to him, "Is your wife or your son nearby so I could talk to them instead?"

You Don't Have to Fulfill the Stereotypes

This kind of reaction by the receptionist is disheartening because very often people just take it for granted that we can't be right because we're older, but it doesn't have to be that way. The good news is that we *can* take responsibility. It's up to this generation of older people to redefine what it means to be old. We don't have to fulfill stereotypes that may have applied to earlier times.

When we refuse to act out or think according to the stereotype, we create very different realities for ourselves. We are the age we believe ourselves to be. It means that we can think positively about ourselves and about our age.

Let me repeat that our worst enemy is ourselves. You can unknowingly send a lot of messages to yourself that are destructive and contrary to achieving success.

You and I have the power to change that. When you catch yourself saying something negative like "Oh, gosh, I'm having a senior moment," you're not really having a senior moment. You're having brain clutter. You need to get that spam, all those negative thoughts, out of your mind.

How often do we say, "I wish I could do that"?

We don't think of that as being negative or limiting, but in fact it is. What we're saying is, "I couldn't do that." I suggest (and I know it works because I do it, and other people do it) that every time you catch yourself saying something negative, immediately turn it around. Put it into a positive and say it out loud with a smile.

"I can do anything I set my mind to."

"I can do anything I want to."

Practice the act of transforming your thoughts and your language because nobody is a worse enemy then we are to ourselves. All we need to do is to listen to ourselves and transform the negative messages into positive ones to wipe that spam out of our minds. We do it on our computer, so we might just as well do it in our brains.

Befriend Younger People

The saying, "We are at the age we believe ourselves to be" is meant to impart this mental attitude. It's so important to recognize that we tend to take on the mannerisms, the talk, and the energy of the people we associate with.

This is why intergenerational relationships are so important. You need as many young friends as you have older friends or friends of your own age. We need to be able to associate with people who are like we are and like we want to be, who are vital and who challenge our thinking, who don't just let us sit there and feel comfortable about what's going on in the world.

They ask pertinent questions, and they challenge us on what we take to be even proper ethics or values. Maybe I'm not going to change my thoughts, but I need to be provoked like that because it's part of staying mentally agile and alert.

Think about all the communities in our country that are 55+, meaning one member of the couple must be at least 55 to live there. Our Florida home is in an intergenerational community. We like seeing young parents and their kids. What would it be like to live without the sound of children laughing and playing? This is part of having regular contact with people of several generations rather than only those in their senior years.

Yale University and the American Institute on Aging have done a study that found some good news about people who are engaged in life, people who think positively, who have a purpose or some reason to go someplace, and positive excitement. These people live on an average of **7 ½** years longer that those who have less enthusiasm for life. They're going to be healthier. They choose to look outside of themselves.

There is research on older people that has discovered the relationship you have with older people when you are a child also is going to influence how positively and healthfully you age. This touches the intergenerational aspect. This touches the positivity. It's all tied together, and it's all in our control because we can control our minds.

This so relates to people who are considering starting a legal nurse consultant business, are thinking about how to expand their business, or how long they wish to continue to practice as a legal nurse consultant, whether self-employed or working as an employee. If you have in your mind a fixed end, i.e., "At the age of 65 I can no longer contribute, I'm longer of value, I will no longer be able to work," then that will influence how you approach your life.

It's one of the reasons that so many people when they retire do one of two things. They either die, or they do what they have always wanted to do. They start a business. They go into gardening. It really is the golden opportunity for people to finally be able to step into their own light, their own joy, own passion, and to do what they would really like to be doing.

CHAPTER 13

How to Build Confidence as an LNC

Self-esteem and self-confidence are intimately connected with business success. I find that some LNCs struggle with self-confidence. There are two ways to build confidence. One is *unintentionally,* and one is *intentionally.* Whether or not it's intentional, the result is the same. You end with a confidence level that really cannot be rattled by a negative outcome, an outcome that was less than favorable, or by another person's criticism.

I've noticed the impact of negative events and people on my self-confidence. I've made some deliberate decisions which contributed to my success. Here is what has worked for me.

1. Limit or if possible, eliminate negative people from your life. These are people who will say, "You know, you're crazy to try this, you'll never succeed." The term for those people is "dream stealers." *Avoid them.* They'll step on your enthusiasm and make you stop before you can even start a business, expand your business, or take on other activity that involves risk. Negative people are one of the biggest destructive forces to entrepreneurs. As I covered in chapter 2, entrepreneurs are *such* a different breed. We have big dreams; we take more risks; we want to do something big; we want to step out. A lot of people don't *ever* do that.

2. Be aware of the risks of listening to all this negative talk. All business owners make mistakes and *achieve unintended outcomes*. You *are* going to fail at something. You're going to take wrong turns; that's part of the journey. But if we're listening to all this negative talk, the first time we fall we'll think, "Maybe they're right, maybe I can't do that." Do you see how that starts your own fear process going? And how that can erode confidence and self-esteem?

3. Surround yourself with positive people. Entrepreneurs understand the mindset of another entrepreneur wanting to do something big, of taking that risk to achieve this big goal, of doing something big and amazing in this world. We need to be surrounded by other entrepreneurs.

Do You Embrace or Avoid Risks?

Do you consider the risks of being a business owner? Do they invigorate you or paralyze you? Some people love risk. Others are risk-averse.

I read an article written by a nurse who decided her way of managing her stress was to go sky diving. The title of the article was perfect: "Never jump out of a perfectly good airplane", a phrase used in "Point Blank." She found she got a rash every time she contemplated going sky diving. I've worked on a few cases involving parachute accidents with bad endings. I know I'll never get a rash because I'll *never* jump out of a perfectly good airplane.

Planning for Risks

How did you plan for risks? Any business involves some degree of risk. Take one phase, for example. Many legal nurse consultants advise a conservative approach to starting a legal nurse consulting business, "Don't quit your day job." Continue your full-time job while you start your legal nurse consulting business, and then ease out of your full-time job. Or take a part-time job and use the remaining days of the week to market. One of the nurses I am mentoring is doing just that. Life care planners may find it easier to take on cases without giving up a clinical job.

What are you willing to risk? Depending on how you start your company, you may need to invest substantial amounts of money on education, mentoring, marketing, and setting up your business. Do you have enough savings to last if you cut yourself off from income and jump right into getting clients?

I talked to one LNC who quit his day job before he had a single client and then found it took longer than he expected to get clients. We discussed the need to return to clinical nursing until he could build up a client base.

The Best Laid Plans...

If you are married, how supportive is your spouse? How secure is his or her job? When I was partway through my master's degree, my husband lost his job. The money we had been about to spend to buy land supported us for a year while I finished my education. For an entire year we did not use a deposit slip. We had *no* income.

When I graduated from my master's degree program, we had $120 in the bank. Luckily, I had a job lined up which I began a few days later. A year later, my husband started his own business, which failed after 3 years, and we narrowly avoided having to declare bankruptcy. I know a thing or two about risks.

How far are you willing to go to establish your business? How much time will you spend; how much discomfort will you endure? The process of learning something new is always accompanied by discomfort. The process of risking can be exhilarating – or uncomfortable.

Benjamin Franklin said, **"Most men die at 21. We just don't bury them until age 60 or 70."** Are you willing to take risks to have a better life, or will you be like my husband's friend, who has been saying for the last 25 years, "Someday I will start my business." Now he is retired from his job. He will *never* start a business.

Nothing will remove all risk from your life. There is risk in being an employee and being laid off. There is risk in crossing the street. Entrepreneurs love the headiness of overseeing their business, and of taking calculated risks. Is your fear of risk holding you back?

One of the best ways to increase your self-esteem is to be successful as an LNC, however you define your success. I encourage you to go out and try.

CHAPTER 14

Exposing LNC Fears: What are You Afraid of?

Fear holds many legal nurse consultants and life care planners back from taking risks in their businesses. If you experience fear, what can you do to help you with your fears? You've got to find something to help you get over this emotion.

Let's examine what this fear means. The ability to fight it is the underpinning to building a positive mindset, the self-esteem, and the confidence that you need to be truly successful. Fear will paralyze us and make it impossible for us to act because we do not know where to head. We need to stop and uncover what it is that we're afraid of; we also need to go back and find out where that fear originated and learn how to subdue it.

We develop these thought and belief patterns when we are very young. If we're told as youngsters that we're brilliant, smart, or funny, that message becomes our belief about ourselves. We're going to act out in ways that support our belief. We're going to act funny; we're going to act smart;

we're going to act special; we're going to act as if we are attractive, whatever we've been told.

If we've been taught the opposite of that, we're going to act out that way. If you are told you have nothing important to say, you're going to turn that into a belief and you're going to act that way. This is not a conscious process. It's totally unconscious, but that is what happens.

Self-worth Drives Legal Nurse Consultants' Fears

It really comes down to self-worth. Ask yourself, "Why am I afraid? What am I afraid of? What happened in my past that has validated this is something to be afraid of, and what can I do to get out of the state of fear so that I can take my business/career to the next level?"

1. Have you received messages from family, friends, or foes that eroded your self-esteem? Were you bullied? Abused? Put down?

2. Are you afraid of a business failure? Are you afraid of the embarrassment of having to admit that you failed?

3. Are you afraid that you're not good enough to help attorneys, no matter what your education?

You'll never entirely get rid of your fears, and honestly, I don't want you to. Fear is an important emotion when you handle it right. Your brain is there to protect you from harm, by any means necessary. Just like nursing rules are there to protect anyone from harm.

Fear, like all emotions, is powerful and neutral. Your fears can work against you, causing you to procrastinate and not fully explore how to succeed in your business. Or, your fear can work for you, pointing out areas for improvement or delegation so you can keep moving forward.

What is Fear?

Dina Eisenberg, an attorney, shares her definition of a fear – it is a negative prediction you are making about an outcome. Fear is the way your brain gets your attention and keeps you safe.

Your fears could be:

- I am no good.
- I will get tripped up when I testify.
- I will not get enough clients to be able to grow my business.
- I can't stay on top of technology trends.
- Where will I find the time to do all of this?

When you encounter negative self-talk, congratulations! You are onto something great that feels risky.

Part of you is saying "no, no, no", while your heart and brain are saying "yes, yes, yes, I'm excited about this".

That's the tension that causes the negative prediction. They can't both be right, right?

A best practice for moving forward with the least amount of stress and drama is to find out what would make it easier for you to say yes to whatever it is your heart desires.

Your fears can paralyze you and lead to a self-destructive depression.

Goal Setting for Legal Nurse Consultants

There are many ways that legal nurse consultants reduce their fears and develop self-confidence. The best way to build confidence is to have the backing of a plan. This way you can get to exactly where you're trying to go. You're reliant on each baby step that you take. Set goals. We understand how to set goals for patients. Do we apply the same process to our business?

A goal is very specific; you can measure it. You may set up a graph and keep track of your results. What can you measure? Here are just a few items:

1. Make 20 marketing calls each week
2. Send out 25 mailings each week
3. Gain 3 new clients per month
4. Convert 75% of potential cases into actual cases
5. Send out 100 invoices this year

6. Reduce invoices that are 30 days past due by 50%

7. Spend no more than 5 hours to locate an expert witness

Legal nurse consultants' goals should be attainable. Many times, we set goals that are unrealistic and not attainable. That sets us up for failure and is another way to totally diminish our confidence and self-esteem. We need to make sure that they're attainable and the time we're allowing ourselves is realistic. Goals should be specific. We should be able to define what we expect to achieve.

Write Specific Goals to Reduce Your Legal Nurse Consultant Fears

You might want to say something like "I feel incredibly empowered, encouraged, and optimistic knowing that I have completed 20 sales calls every week for the last 90 days that have resulted in 45 new conversations and 18 new clients."

That's your legal nurse consulting business goal, but you're writing it as if it's already happened. Do you see how specific it is? It's specific about the timeframe and about the quantity of calls. You could even add a revenue number into that goal because where the mind focuses, the mind goes.

Every step brings you closer to the big goal, when you start to experience that feeling of personal and financial freedom, of fearlessness, of being empowered, of knowing who you are, of having strength and choice in your life as well as control of your life. Set your goals high so they stretch you, but realistically, so that you can grow and enjoy the accomplishment.

Set quarterly goals. Break them into steps with specific deadlines. Then review your quarterly goals at least every other week, adjust deadlines, and highlight those that are accomplished. Enjoy the process of accomplishing your goals. Use your quarterly goals to energize and focus you to appreciate what you have accomplished.

Goal setting by legal nurse consultants reduces fears and helps you move your legal nurse consulting business forward. Start today.

Think of Goals as Short Term and Long Term, a Model We Understand from Nursing

Short term goals break the big goal into tiny steps, so we don't get overwhelmed with the big goal. We get encouraged and gain momentum by achieving the small goals. Every step brings you closer to the big goal. You start to experience a feeling of personal and financial freedom, of fearlessness, of being empowered, of having strength and choice in your life as well as control of your life. Set your goals high so they stretch you. But make them realistic so that you can grow and enjoy the accomplishment.

Set Quarterly Goals

Break them into steps. I set quarterly goals with specific deadlines, which I reviewed with my staff at least every other week, adjusted deadlines, and highlighted those we accomplished. We enjoyed marking these as done. The quarterly goals energized and focused us and helped us appreciate what we accomplished.

CHAPTER 15

How to Tackle Limiting Beliefs

We all hear a lot about the importance of making good choices. If two different careers or jobs present themselves as possibilities, we know we must choose between them. We choose spouses, places to live, and political candidates. As legal nurse consultants, we make choices about accepting and refusing clients, employees, and analyzing cases.

It may seem to us that we make these choices freely, and if our choices give us positive results, we don't question them. However, sometimes our choices boomerang, and we suffer from their results. We ask ourselves how we could have made such bad decisions.

In contrast, people may think they have no choices at all. They have no idea how strongly they can affect their own lives. They may wake up each day prepared to battle with circumstances. A favorite expression of such people is, "These are the cards that I was dealt."

Whether we believe we're operating by free choice or that we don't have choices, we're unaware of the invisible system that drives us to make both our positive and our negative decisions or to decide that we are choice less.

You may have heard of this perspective as locus of control. Those with an external locus of control believe they are not in charge of their life or their health. Internal locus of control people believe the opposite. Entrepreneurs function very much within the internal locus of control view.

The Beliefs Systems That Limit Us

A mindset is a fixed understanding that you believe in (usually without knowing it) and support with thoughts and actions. It's basically your belief system. Everybody has one.

A colleague of mine woke up to realize she had a failed marriage, a house in foreclosure, a debt of $40,000, and a car in repossession. She was a well-paid professional, but she was living oblivious to her role in creating the circumstances crashing around her. In living by the philosophy of taking each day as it came, she had neglected to recognize that sometimes, like tsunamis, everything came at once. Feeling overwhelmed, she attempted suicide.

Today she says forthrightly that her mindset created those circumstances and drove her to that decision. If you want to know what your mindset is doing for you or where it's limiting you, look at the circumstances you're in. She says that when she woke up on that bathroom floor, she heard, "You are the common denominator," meaning that she was the one who was making all the choices in her life.

She asked herself, "If I'm making these choices, and these are the results I'm getting, what do I need to know about me that will help me make different choices to bring about other results?" Like many other people have done, she realized that she could turn her mindset into something that produced much better results than broken relationships, issues around money, and stumbling through life.

Beliefs Determine Results

We all succeed in getting results that match our beliefs, our mindset. Beliefs determine the results we're going to have. If you believe that you can't fight City Hall as my father told me when I was growing up, City Hall will win every time.

As legal nurse consultants and life care planners, we've had countless opportunities to witness how differently people recover from virtually identical injuries. Think of a person who gets into a car crash and ends up with multiple fractures. There can be a downward spiral in that person's life. The car is gone. The job is gone. The role has changed. If the injured person was the breadwinner, he or she can longer bring in income. The person stays home, is depressed, and gains weight.

Same Circumstances, Different Results

Yet other people with the same types of injuries never get caught in this vicious cycle. They have a completely different course. They figure out how to overcome their obstacles. They figure out how to get a job that's consistent with their new physical realities. They participate actively in rehab. They get stronger, and they get back on their feet.

Another example might be two people who have made millions of dollars in the stock market. The stock market crashes, and one of those people goes on and makes millions more dollars. The other person commits suicide, or goes into depression, and gives up.

You can have someone who is very successful, earns a lot of money, and who will continue to always be successful. You can take a person who's poor and sees himself as a victim. No matter how much money you give them, in time, they're right back to poverty. In such cases, you will find that the mindset of "I am a victim" determines the results.

This issue around mindset affects us in every aspect of our lives. Returning to the example of the two injured people who approach their circumstances in such diverse ways, their belief systems determine their response mechanisms, and their abilities to respond to new conditions and new sets of circumstances.

A breadwinner who goes through that kind of an injury and can no longer provide for the family finds one of his or her limiting beliefs activated. This belief will filter the way he or she views life.

Where You Left the Keys

A very simple and mundane example of this relates to lost keys. Imagine that you're looking for your keys on a table close to the front door. Someone comes in and asks why you're looking for them there, since they obviously aren't on the table. You say, "But that's where I always put them."

Because your belief filter says the keys belong there, you don't look anywhere else. A more significant belief filter, such as, "People like me don't get good-paying clients" will direct you to low-paying clients even if good-paying clients are available. You'll sabotage your success.

Some beliefs hide for years or decades. The two people who were injured probably never had to deal with severe physical conditions. Once they are living with them, their minds go through their belief systems and filter the appropriate beliefs.

They may both have strong feelings about not being able to provide for their families. One person may have additional beliefs about his being a hopeless situation. "You could never come back from such an injury." This leads to feelings of failure, shame, and defeat. He gives up. The other has this belief: "Nothing is impossible to those who are dedicated." She is determined to find a way for herself and her family to thrive. She has a strong and motivating goal.

I once worked on a case involving a girl who was injured on a soccer field and developed osteomyelitis in her bone.

She fought unsuccessfully for two years to keep her leg. Then, when she was 23, it was amputated. She became a strong advocate for people who had amputated limbs. She became active in an organization that supports people who are amputees. She found a purpose and a meaning.

She was happier once the agony of trying to save her leg was over and adjusted to her new reality, but she could have said, "Nobody will ever love me. I'll never be attractive. My life is over because I've lost my leg." Her belief system of about herself did not contain those thoughts.

We Form Our Beliefs Early in Life

During the first seven years of our lives, we develop our beliefs about ourselves, the basic core established beliefs about what we're good at, what we can do, what we cannot do, how smart we are, and many other beliefs. This young woman had developed a very strong belief about who she was.

Her self-esteem was established as being one who was not affected by her body. When this injury occurred, she initially tried to keep her leg, which is totally understandable. When she gave up the limb, no belief activated that said her being without a limb equaled, "I'm not good enough," "I'm not loved," "I'm unlovable," or "I'm no longer beautiful."

Because she didn't have that established, her response was relief and joy. She went on to do important things with her life and to be a very happy person. Her courage and dedication illustrate that we establish who we are.

We Make It Up

When we're small children, we're trying to figure out who we are. We look for clues. A lot of information comes from our parents, who may say, "She's shy." "She's good with people." "She's no good at sports."

This information is being directed at us, but we still choose what we believe or don't believe. Maybe we think sports are boring and saying we're no good at them is a clever way of getting out of playing. We decide what's true about us, but because we make these decisions when we're so young, we forget and think they're true.

Returning once again to those two injured people, when they were much younger, they adopted certain beliefs that determined how they responded to their altered conditions. One ended up disempowered; the other ended up moving forward.

Mindset for Legal Nurse Consultants and Life Care Planners

Take the example of two legal nurses. Each is responsible for marketing, calling on, and selling herself to the attorney. One individual has a mindset of beliefs that she could sell ice to an Eskimo. The other's mindset says, "I can't sell anything."

The one who can sell anything will be able to pick up the phone and book the appointments. She will be able to walk in and establish instant rapport with the attorney, who will be eager to hire her.

The one who believes she couldn't sell anything, with possible additional beliefs that she's not good enough, will develop symptomatic behavior of finding lots of "good" reasons why she can't make the sales calls or why she can't go out and meet with the attorney.

These kinds of limiting beliefs are very painful. People who have them get fearful or upset, worried and angry. They may also feel guilty, and they may resent other nurses who can do what they can't.

These emotions are response mechanisms to the mindset of their inability to go out and make the sales. The development of their business will be highly limited in terms of what they can do. The issue is that they really don't know what's behind their belief system. They don't know about these filters. They don't even know that they exist, much less that the filters keep all their beliefs in alignment.

If "I'm not good enough" is one of those beliefs, they won't be able to call an attorney because their mindset will be that they're not qualified or that the attorney knows more. It will always prevent them from being able to reach the level of developing friendly relationships with lawyers and working well with them. It will limit them in any aspect of their job performance.

They're going to find reasons like, "I don't have my website up yet, I don't know how to exhibit at a conference, I don't know how to do the marketing page, I don't know how to do a newsletter" or whatever marketing techniques that someone is coaching them in. They will use those excuses to keep from approaching the sales aspect of their business.

A legal nurse consultant struggling to get clients told me she could not be successful because she was not married to an attorney. In her belief system, only LNCs with attorney spouses or boyfriends would be successful in this field. I can count on one hand the LNCs I know who are in these relationships!

How to Shift Your Mindset

Begin by realizing that the way you think determines the way you speak, and that will always determine what your results are going to be.

Look at the thoughts that you're having. What are the actions that you are taking? What actions do you think you are *incapable* of taking because of the thoughts you have? What do you think you *can* do?

You can ask yourself, "Why don't I want to make this phone call?" Be honest with yourself when you answer. If you think, "I'm afraid," don't be ashamed. There are no wrong or bad answers.

Ask yourself, "Why am I afraid?" This question may take you to childhood. Countless people are afraid to speak up because someone made fun of them when they had to give a speech or report in front of a class. Some kids were bullied or had parents who told them, "Children should be seen and not heard."

Whatever you come up is a belief, not a truth. The best thing about beliefs is that they can be changed. And when you change your *beliefs*, you change your *circumstances.*

If you're not sure of this, again return to your clinical experience. What is true about the differences between patients in terms of who thrives and who doesn't applies to your life. If you learned to believe that you weren't resilient and couldn't change your circumstances, you can change that belief. It's all a matter of mindset.

We can all benefit from looking at our limiting beliefs, our mindset, and the way that we speak about our goals and our intentions, and our vision for ourselves. We can believe that there are alternatives.

CHAPTER 16

How to Keep Stepping Up Your Business Success

You've heard the expression that no one likes change except for a wet baby. Because change is inevitable and necessary for everyone, we need to have a more positive perspective on it. Business owners need to focus on the positive aspects of change.

Some key principles can help us both in the calm and rough periods of our lives and to successfully navigate change.

Self-Management, Self-Leadership, and Self-Mastery

Self-management means tuning into situations, so you can understand them more clearly, and making that engagement effective to get the best possible results. It's really an introductory level to your self-awareness, as I outlined in the previous chapter.

Self-leadership involves looking at the way you can stretch yourself. You examine how you use your skills. You look at how you respond to the way other people react to you.

That leads to self-mastery, which is the height of self-awareness. At that stage, we're looking at even softer skills, the way we serve each other, and the way people react to us when we serve. It relates to how thankful we are in situations, our gratitude levels, and whether our desires really match what we want people to recognize us for. Those three areas are key for you to be able to face any kind of situation and handle it well and to come out feeling fulfilled and purposeful.

Fulfilling Your Purpose

Fulfillment and being able to master your purpose is a key aspect of being able to effectively handle a business. Legal nurse consultants are generally either employees working in law firms or insurance companies or self-employed and working directly with attorneys who are either plaintiff attorneys or defense attorneys. Life care planners are usually self-employed.

We can be put in situations where we question our potential. We might, for example, be asked to take on a new kind of difficult case. Or we could be asked to serve as an expert witness and provide testimony in court. We may question, "Am I good enough? Am I up to the challenge that's being given to me?" I recall how terrified I was when I learned I had to go to court to testify as an expert. My adrenaline skyrocketed. It was an important first step in what became a 20-year-long role as a liability expert witness.

Potential is born in every single one of us, but few of us reach the full potential that is put within us. At the start of our careers, we sometimes know what we want and sometimes don't, but we push it as far as we can, and then we settle within the boundaries we've set.

Only by focusing on your potential and being willing to realize it can you stretch and push the boundaries. When you push those boundaries, you can start to build new skills that will take you to the next level, but to push those boundaries, you need to act.

The steps that we take define the people we become. They also define the work that we do. It's important that we continue to take steps and push the boundaries so that we can start to see some of the skills that we have residing within us that would otherwise have remained hidden.

I've seen people, including myself, who get very uncomfortable when they push beyond their boundaries or they are being pushed by some force to take on new responsibilities or to do uncomfortable things. You've probably been in that situation, and you may have wished you knew how to handle that intense discomfort.

Accept the Challenge

When you're being stretched, it's important to rise to the challenge involved. The stretch will do this for you: It will help you to develop more competence in the area that you currently work. It will sharpen your skill if you lean towards it instead of shrinking from it. Our confidence is increased if we're willing to stretch those boundaries. It isn't a comfortable place, but that place of stretch is where growth happens. It's important that we take steps through it to get to the next level and to get to the next place.

I can remember a time in my life when I was very concerned about a family relative who I thought had some mental illness. I sat in front of a phone with the phone number for the hotline for the local mental health service. I remember staring at that phone thinking, "When I reach out and touch that phone it's going to change my life."

I had to force myself to make the call. It was probably one of the most difficult phone calls that I ever made because it meant that I had to acknowledge there was a problem I needed help with. The call resulted in my husband and me taking a course that gave us coping skills, strategies, and information to be able to handle this relative to make a real positive change in our relationship.

Turn Disasters into Direction

If we can turn our disasters into direction, they will serve us going forward. We must experience those tough times to know how to address them because challenges *will* come. This is part of life. The more we have experienced it and the more that we've been able to step through it and step up to the change, the more we provide ourselves with skills that we can use in our lives.

We may feel that we prefer for our lives to be on a nice, steady plateau or going up towards positive things, but it's often what you learn in the trough on the other side of the mountain that tests you and changes you.

The Introvert's Special Challenge

One of the activities that stretches legal nurse consultants is the act of engaging in networking and meeting people. This is especially challenging to introverts (which I am) and shy people who need to go into a social setting, actively network, and connect and talk to people. I know that there are extroverts who don't struggle with that and might not even be able to identify with that feeling.

Over my many years of networking, I've reach an understanding of what will help introverts (and will do extroverts no harm to practice). Networking is a challenging experience for anyone who doesn't really like talking to strangers. I've noticed that many people approach it by being in the room for what *they* can get and for how they can tell people about what they want.

Consider this alternate approach. What if you change how you view the experience? Instead of talking at people about yourself, seek to really listen to them. This shifted the networking experience for me. By taking the focus off myself, by not trying to talk to other people about myself, I also reduced my anxiety about myself and how I appeared. I built better relationships than I had previously once I decided to engage with people. I also learned to give myself breaks or time to decompress after a particularly stimulating day.

If we approach the networking as we really are, we don't need to put on any airs and graces. We don't really need to impress. People want to connect with you, the person. It's you they will remember, not your grand title. They will remember how you engaged with them. They will remember how you treated them.

Also bear in mind that if you show interest by asking other people questions about themselves, they perceive you as being a wonderful conversationalist. This makes you stand out from the crowd because many people just don't do that. It's easier to stand out by not doing what everybody else is doing.

Requesting Referrals

Another thing that stretches legal nurse consultants is asking for referrals at such networking events. They are there primarily to find attorneys who can hire them. The people in the networking event may know attorneys, but they may be standing and looking at a legal nurse consultant trying to figure out, "Do I know this person, do I like this person, do I trust this person? Should I connect her with the attorneys I know?"

Consider that this isn't the best way to get referrals. The idea of wanting referrals by just handing a business card over or introducing yourself and giving a name, a title and perhaps a little background about what you do is not normal. That's not generally how people react to each other. Be prepared to build the relationship. Be prepared to do more than just meet people in the room.

Ultimately, you want to build a relationship that goes beyond the room that you're in at the time. When you're first meeting and getting to know someone, it's premature to make that kind of request. Instead, once you've made a connection with someone, you can go home and drop them a quick email saying, "You know it's been really good to connect with you."

When you make a good connection, you might arrange to meet for coffee at another time. You can refer to that in your email. If that doesn't happen, have a conversation or a phone call. This make for a private rather than a public interaction.

In that setting, talk about how you can help each other. This might involve you asking for a referral but wait until you find out how you can help them, as well. Instead of getting caught up in how they can help you, ask how you can help them first.

This keeps you from getting caught up in the mindset of who do you know and who can you *refer me* to instead of who do you want to know and who can I *connect you with*. Asking first what you can do to assist the other is crucial. Being generous to another person inspires generosity on their part. The saying, "As you sow, so shall you reap" fully applies.

The Importance of Optimism

Optimism is one of the key ingredients to being successful in a business. I have talked to lots of LNCs who are not optimistic about their businesses. They've gone through some training and then found it tougher to locate clients than they expected. They are really filled with pessimism and have given up or are sometimes in despair. They have spent a lot of money. They have announced that they want this business and then they find it tough.

It's always good to be looking for the next thing, the next connection, the way ahead, and where you want to be. This means having an element of hope in your life, which ties into optimism. You've got to expect the best for yourself and for the people who you're working with, even the people who you live with. You've got to expect the best, and to do that, optimism is going to be key.

I'm fully convinced that you need optimism to succeed. I note that people have the right to be as pessimistic as they want to be, but do you want to be around them? Do you want to do business with them? As I've mentioned elsewhere in this book, I try to keep negative people out of my life.

Negative people aren't going to attract the kinds of people who they want in their lives. It's important that we somehow find a way to train our minds to think more positively, to train our minds to be hopeful.

Two ways to do this are daily meditation and dwelling on the things that are going to help you, things that bring life into you. Cultivate the attitude of expecting good things to happen during the day.

Choose Your Attitude

You have choices. You *can* choose to think, "Nothing is going to happen today. I'm going to go into this networking meeting, and I'm not going to make any connections."

Speaking for myself, why would I bother going if that's what I expect? I need to be expecting more than that. It is a mindset, and that a different mindset is needed, one that is open to change and open to the opportunities that might come your way. A closed mind operates in pessimism.

When you open your mind, you invite success. An open mind enables you to recover from the setbacks that come your way. An optimist can see a setback and think, "This is where I am now; where do I want to be?" You need an element of hope in your life.

A business can have great highs, things that go very well. It can also have negative experiences which you must be able to bounce back from. For example, when you testify as an expert witness, you are deposed, and then you go to trial if the case doesn't settle. You can testify very well in

10, 15, or 20 trials and then you have an experience that makes you want to sink through the floor and disappear.

You must be able to get up at the end of that period, walk out of the courtroom, and know that it is a quirk. It's an aberrancy. You want to be able to determine if you did something that related to not feeling good when you left that courtroom. Be optimistic enough to realize the next experience doesn't have to be that same way. The next experience can be wonderful. You need to be able to bounce back from a negative experience or feeling.

This ability is tied in with the way that you see the world. Optimists have a much better chance of being able to pull themselves out of that than a pessimist does.

Handling Major Change

In our world there could be a key customer who stopped giving work to a legal nurse consultant, or a key attorney in a law firm who decides to retire or is no longer in practice for another reason. That can change the legal nurse consultant's world in significant ways. Changes in the law can make a certain type of case no longer profitable to pursue. A nurse may have been counting on those types of cases to keep her business going.

How can we use change as an opportunity to look at our attitude? How can we look at those tremendous changes, learn from them, and focus in on what we need to do in our heads to deal with those things?

You may have noticed that some people who go through difficult circumstances or situations are able to bounce back, as I described in the previous chapter on limiting beliefs. Others go through it, and they're stuck. The foundation of either attitude and action approach is your attitude.

You Are Not Your Circumstances

Attitude has everything to do with how happy we are. We can't derive our level of happiness from the circumstances that we go through. Circumstances happen. If they're what determine how okay you feel and whether you can go on with life very well, you're likely to sink and sink very fast.

You need to have a separation between how you feel and the circumstances that come your way. Your attitude about what happens will determine whether you come out of it well or whether you sink. The real power in having a good attitude is the understanding that whatever you're going through now is not the end. It will change, and it will pass. Things can be different if you will just keep stepping through. You will step up to what needs to happen, and you're prepared to do what it takes to get to the next level.

Your attitude should always be that this circumstance happened, but this isn't necessarily who I am. Tomorrow is a different day. Things can be different. It's important to have that kind of thinking particularly when you're going through challenging times.

If we can see changes and opportunity, change can mean approaching it differently. It could mean having a different mindset about the circumstance you're in. It doesn't have to be a momentous change that may cause you to leave this job and go somewhere else. It sometimes calls for a shift in the way we think about where we are right now.

You can really have joy wherever you are, in any situation, however difficult. You can have something that you can be thinking of that is better than where you are now.

My son has a business called "Ever New Joy" and the one thing that he tells me every time I finish talking to him or leave him he'll say, "Have fun."

The words that we speak to ourselves are so important. Who is the first person to hear what comes out of your mouth? It's you, so whatever you say, whatever you speak out, or whatever it is you're going to read, make sure it's uplifting. Make sure it's good for you. Make sure it gives you a pleasant life so that you can take your steps with lightness and joy.

CHAPTER 17

Finding Joy Leads to Business Success

Happiness is a skill. It's a research-proven science in the field of positive psychology. There are many different techniques people can use to help them with stress, to feel more confident, productive, focused, and they're making a difference, that they matter.

There are different skills such as gratitude, mindfulness, and self-compassion that people use during their busy days. This could involve having a purposeful pause before you send an email to an attorney who might be your next client.

Checking in with yourself, being grateful for what you have, and how far you've come along might be enough to boost your confidence and be able to then take the next step, which is making the phone call.

The Gift of Gratitude

Focusing on gratitude is an instant happiness booster. When we're happy, our energy goes up. When our energy goes up, other things go up, like our ability to feel confident, to concentrate, to speak articulately, to feel more inviting, more attractive, and more magnetic to other people.

We can use simple gratitude skills. Your trigger could be as little as being grateful for arriving to work five minutes earlier or perhaps getting recognition from an attorney client about something that you did. Anything that falls under the category of gratitude can help people feel better. When you feel better, you're able to produce and be more productive. Your performance goes up.

A simple technique of gratitude has a positive ripple effect in many areas you may touch upon that day.

One of my coaches shared a daily practice with me. At the end of every day, he writes five or six lines of things that happened for which he's grateful. You can make this practice even more powerful by writing a reason why you're grateful for those things, events or people.

We could be in a state of gratitude for our spouse or our children. We can say that repeatedly. "I'm grateful for my spouse. I'm grateful for my home. I'm grateful for my kids." What if we take the time and ask ourselves, "Why am I grateful for my spouse today? What did he or she do or what quality does this person have that I'm grateful for?" That really challenges us to dig deeper into why we're grateful. That's the booster of the positive emotion. It makes it last longer.

I say aloud five things I'm grateful for every single day. That helps me to focus on what's so good in life because there are so many remarkable things happening. In addition, you can keep such a list on your computer or in a journal. This list could also include simple things like "I got a great parking space for my appointment today." I'm always happy about that. It's whatever makes sense for you. Keep paying attention to things that are working.

If you think about people you know, you'll notice that for many the default is to think about what went wrong, what negative things happened in their lives today. I've discovered from studying negative people at a distance (because I try to keep them far away) that the negativity they exude is contagious.

You can switch that and say, "How can I be positive?" "What am I grateful for?" What went well today?"

"The sun shone. I was able to get out in my pool yesterday and submerge up to my neck. I took a walk on the road, and a deer crossed my pathway." Those are all the things I'm grateful for.

By focusing on gratitude, you can reduce your stress. Flip through that gratitude journal periodically and remind yourself of all the things you have you might take for granted.

Those who regularly practice gratitude report it has helped them deal with issues and problems. The more one practices gratitude, the more one sees how it shapes all aspects of life and your business.

Think of gratitude as being related to appreciation. That which appreciates grows.

Dealing with the Special Stresses of Litigation

You work with high-stakes cases and often with demanding clients who have a great deal of stress associated with how they're handling their cases.

If a plaintiff attorney takes the wrong case, for example, and ends up spending $50,000 or $100,000 on it and losing it because it wasn't a winnable case to begin with, that creates a lot of stress. If a defense attorney is working with an insurance carrier, and the insurance carrier is not happy with the results that the defense attorney is getting, the carrier can yank all the cases away from the law firm.

There's a lot of tension associated with how cases are handled, conclusions that legal nurse consultants reach, how much they bill for their services, and whether that amount is perceived to be a realistic amount. When your clients are stressed, that in turn generates a lot of stress on you.

Get Enough Sleep

One of the best ways to handle any stress is to take preventive measures. Set yourself up for success by getting enough sleep. It does make an enormous difference because when we wake up tired, we arrive at work stressed already or tired. We're not at our best.

When we are fully rested, we're able to take a step back from the situation and not automatically become more reactive. We're able to have a chance to respond more clearly or be able to see a different angle in how to handle certain situations, how to approach the person or the company a little bit better. Sleep is very important.

Create an Intention

I have had success with another preventive technique called creating an intention. Before you go to sleep, create the intention that you're going to wake up fully rested. When you wake up, create the intention that you're going to have a good day. When you create that intention, your mind will do its best to make that happen. A good day is going to be different every day, but when we make a declaration, we are in the best situation to be in alignment for that intention.

I believe in a lot of preventive ways of managing stress because once we're involved in our business, we're going to be pulled in so many different directions. The more we can arm ourselves with simple nourishing skills that are going to help us pre-pave our day, the more powerful and confident we will be that day.

You will discover that life looks easier when you're well rested and you're not running on that ragged nerve.

The Five Rs

Debbie Lyn Toomey, a nurse, who trains companies and organizations in how to use happiness skills to boost their productivity, performance, and relationships, has created a model that helps to release our own superheroes. It's built on five "R" words.

Here are the first 3: Reflect, Remember, and Recognize. We put so much investment in learning legal nurse consulting. We don't take the time to study ourselves. It's very good to just stop, reflect, and think about your life.

Reflect on what you've experienced last year or the last five years, depending on how far back you want to go.

The whole idea is to stop, reflect, and think about all the positive things that have occurred in your life. You can think about obstacles and reflect on what you did in those circumstances that allowed you to rise above them. When you start noticing them, look at the pattern and see which technique and/or strength you used the most in those circumstances.

The more we take the time to reflect, the more likely we are to recognize the patterns. The more we recognize the patterns, the more likely we are to say, "That is me. I do that. That helps me overcome this. That helped me when this happened." The more we remember, the more we'll be likely to learn the lessons of the past.

It also helps to reflect on experiences, recognize and own what you see or what you normally do.

Debbie has a Wonder Woman LEGO keychain. She finds that both fun and a nice reminder that says, "You've got something unique to offer other people to help them become better or make this world a better place." She also employs quotes: "Reflect", "Recognize," and "Remember."

Read. The more we read about our strengths, for example, by keeping and reading a journal or reading our gratitude lists, the more we reinforce our strength and confidence. For many, gratitude is a top-ranking strength. It helps us whether we're having work problems or feeling that we're stuck in dead-end jobs. It can help you go into work in a positive framework, a frame of mind that can allow you to attract your next position.

Reaping. Debbie recommends asking people what they think of you. They can often surprise you by sharing positive qualities you may not believe you have. By hearing this, you reap the benefits.

We're often conditioned to be shy, bashful, and to turn away any compliments or forms of gratitude, appreciation, or recognition that people give us. We say, "Oh no, it's not me. That wasn't really me. It was nothing."

People can say, "You did an excellent job. That was great. I appreciate you doing that. We couldn't have done it without you." Some people will respond with, "No, that wasn't me. It was nothing. I was just lucky." We diminish the impact of what we've accomplished. When we start reaping more of these positive compliments or recognitions, we feel better.

In summary, these are the five:

1. Reflect
2. Recognize
3. Remember
4. Read
5. Reap

Happiness and Productivity

Productivity concerns people who own their businesses. "How much are you getting done?" It seems like when you're in business, there's a never-ending list of things that need to be accomplished.

Happiness has been shown to boost productivity. Anything that brings you happiness will boost your energy in a way that's going to make you feel good about what you're doing, the challenge that you have in front of you, and how you look at yourself.

The more we purposely use happiness for productivity the better. One way to accomplish this is to do something outside of work that helps us feel good. It could be a sport or a hobby that you love. The more you do it, the more you feel good going back into the workplace. It gives you something to look forward to. After you've done it, you feel happy and as if you made effective use of your time. That's productive. For example, I love kayaking in the rivers of Florida. I see wildlife and appreciate the sunshine and views of a world I can never see from the road. At the end of a trip I am tired and refreshed.

Happiness increases our energy, and when our energy goes up, creativity goes up. We become able to see the whole situation in a different light, in the broader scheme of things instead of feeling stuck or trapped in a situation.

Happiness can help us become innovative and do things faster because we don't feel like we're being dragged down or that we are wasting our time. As a mood lifter, it influences our ability to concentrate and to complete the tasks that we've identified.

Be Playful

A study on adults and play revealed that when they engage in a playful activity, they boost their ability to be creative. Their innovation goes up. Their ability to socialize or be engaging goes up. Their productivity and performance go up.

How can that work for legal nurse consultants? It could mean wearing something a little bit different, maybe a playful color that's still businesslike but not what you usually wear. You could wear a bracelet or jewelry that reminds you of something that makes you happy. It could mean something as simple as using a pen that you got from a conference where you met somebody who was really kind and very generous.

You could take a different route to work, learning how to maneuver the traffic in a unique way, and getting there faster. Being creative with play is a booster to our positive emotion.

My son is developing a computer game and is finding that in the mainstream a lot more people are attracted to games that bring them happiness. His game is nonviolent and has a figure that is exploring different universes. In general, the people in the gaming world are upbeat and lively. They love what they do and they're happy. They're fun to be around.

Engage Others

You could invite a colleague to play with you. One example is to share a short and simple exercise of walking up and down stairs. That gets you away from the desk and the office, and, if you're working in a hospital, from patient care.

Having a partner in such activities increases the likelihood that you'll do them, and it's more fun to do it together. You can have fun, chat with each other, and do something positive for body and mind.

Self-Care for Nurses

When I went to nursing school, the focus was understandably on patient care. What was missing was the concept that carers also need to practice self-care.

Now the healthcare industry has changed. Our workload is increasing even more, and the demands are high. Many times, nurses work 12-hour shifts. They go through these shifts without having time to take bathroom or lunch breaks. They'll try to grab a meal while finishing their documentation. They're sacrificing themselves to get the job done. These unhealthy practices make nurses feel resentful, stressed, burned out, and as if they don't matter.

Ignoring self-care is no longer an option. We need to add ourselves to the patient workload. If you have four or five patients, add yourself to the list. That will make you more likely to take care of yourself because we are so list-driven. We need to realize that taking care of ourselves is as important as taking care of our assigned patients. If we don't do that, both the patients and we suffer.

Legal Initiatives

A law firm in the Philadelphia area started filing lawsuits against hospitals because nurses were not being able to take their breaks. They were not being given the equivalent amount of money. They were not being compensated in any way for working straight through for eight or twelve hours without a break.

The attorney in this law firm came up with a theory that the hospitals had to pay back for those breaks that were never granted to the nurses. This attorney systematically went after several major hospitals in the Philadelphia area and was successful with all the suits. The hospitals had to pay lots of money to the nurses in their employ who had not received the breaks that they were entitled to.

The treatment of nurses was bad for the nurses' well-being. The publicity involved in being the target of lawsuits was bad for the hospitals.

Taking Responsibility for Our Well-Being

We nurses need to own the fact that we need to take care of ourselves at work in our business because we can't be martyrs. We cannot afford *not* to take care of ourselves. We need to give ourselves permission to do that. We then need to be able to take our breaks.

Whether you're a full-time LNC or also work in a clinical setting, you can benefit from the practice of happiness and self-appreciation.

Sit back, look, take a deep breath, and appreciate the things that are going well in your life. And don't forget your gratitude list.

CHAPTER 18

Fueling Your Body for Success

One of my legal nurse consulting friends often says, "Your health is your wealth". Focusing on health goals is more challenging than ever because of the way we all have chosen to live and the way that society has developed in the last couple of decades. We're all so incredibly busy. Life has changed dramatically since the invention of the Internet. Because of cell phones, laptops, computers and modern technology, life is hurdling forward at an unprecedented speed. We're not used to this, so we're all multi-tasking.

Health Not a Priority – or is it?

Quite often for those of us who are so incredibly busy our health and our wellbeing are not at the top of our priority list. It's down at the bottom and that's why there is now a whole career opening for health coaches, who sit down with people and help them prioritize in their life. Quite often that means telling them it's okay to take care of yourself. It's almost like we need to give permission these days to put ourselves at the top of the list or at least number two. You must take care of yourself before you can take care of everyone else and your business.

There's so much fast food and unhealthy food. Your food is loaded with sugar and chemicals, things that we don't need. Those are the foods that we often grab when we're on the go.

You must make your health a priority, to think about it and dedicate time to it. Once you do that though, it can become a part of your routine; that's what a health coach does to help you re-prioritize so that your health is not at the bottom of the list. It's at the top.

Small business owners these days quite often are online, so sometimes when they are sleeping, resting or taking care of themselves their business is working, but you're still responsible. You're still the boss. If you are the owner, it starts with you. Nobody has time to be sick these days. Prioritizing your health and making your wellbeing number one is a must.

Weight Control

We know that Americans are becoming larger. I've gone into furniture stores with my son; we're both small people. We've sat in chairs side-by-side and filled the chair, which was meant for one person. We know that in health care there is a whole specialty of bariatric medicine, bariatric stretchers and bariatric services. Why is it so difficult for Americans to control their weight?

The answer is simple. Our food has changed radically; our grocery stores have changed, and our lifestyles have changed. We're all sedentary. We all like to sit in front of laptops and computers all day long to get our work done. That's become our job.

If you shop around the perimeter of the grocery store you're going to be just fine because that's where you're going to find fruits, vegetables, lean meats, fish and seafood. It's when you go up and down the aisles of the grocery store that you're going to get in trouble because there are so much processed and packaged food in our culture.

Restaurants have doubled and tripled portion size. It's the content of our food that matters. It's the size of our food portions. It's the sugar. It's the chemicals. It's the fast food and it's the way we're all living our lives these days. We're over-scheduled.

Most two-person head-of-household families have two people working full-time most of the time. That leaves very little time for proper grocery store shopping, planning for meals or making your health and wellbeing a priority, especially in the nursing world.

If you look back to 100 years ago or 150 years ago, what were people eating? They were growing their food. They were eating food that was sourced locally that they grew, or their neighbors grew. They were eating animals who were feeding behind their home or in the field next to them. It was a very different time and that was long before obesity rates skyrocketed in this country, which really happened after the 50s and the 60s when our food started to change. It became all about convenience.

How to Lose Weight

You know there are many types of weight loss plans. Consider the concept of bio-individuality, which means that what works for me is not necessarily going to work for you. You need to figure out what your best diet is and what works for your body; listen to your body.

What do you crave, what do you like to eat, what works for your body? That's bio-individuality, but we also talk about primary foods and secondary foods. Primary food is not what you would think. *Secondary* food is the food that you put on your plate. That's the food that we consume like fruits, proteins, vegetables, carbohydrates, fats and so on.

Primary food is so much more than that. Your primary food is basically your career, exercise, relationships and spirituality. Those are the things people really need to look at before they spend too much time thinking about what they want to eat.

Look at what's right in your life, what's not quite right and what you should be working on as opposed to what should be on the plate in front of you.

- "Do you like your job or business? Are you where you are supposed to be and is something holding you back there?"

- "Do you have a spirituality practice? Do you need one in your life? Did you used to have one and you got away from it?"

- "Do you have any kind of exercise in your life?"

  Exercise is a big part of weight loss. You may think, "I walk a lot and I get around a lot", but sometimes we fool ourselves into thinking we're active when we're not. We're sedentary.

  These are additional questions:

- "What's going on in your relationships? Are you in a happy marriage? Are you dating somebody who fills you up as opposed to drains you? Do you have a partner who brings out the best in you? Do you bring out the best in your partner? How are you around your kids?"

Primary food is so much more than food. It's looking at the whole picture and not just what goes in your mouth. A lot of people aren't prepared to look at that when they're thinking of starting a "new diet". I like to say, "Eating plan" because you must plan on what you're eating for you to really feed your body. The question most of the time is, "Are you feeding your taste buds, are you feeding your cravings, are you stuffing down your emotions or are you giving your body fuel?"

Think of it this way: You buy yourself a nice car. You get successful. You get yourself a top of the line car that you worked very hard for. You must put premium gasoline in that car to keep it running. Most people would never even consider putting regular gas in that car. The same thing is true of our body. You have been given one body. It is a gift. It is full of things that you need to keep healthy, so why would you put garbage fuel inside of your body?

Add vegetables back into your world. It's so easy to get away from vegetables, but vegetables are the primary fuel along with some fruits, lean meats, proteins and water. It's not that hard to figure out if you just simplify things and you go back to the way things used to be. You eat real food, stay away from the processed stuff and stay away from the sugar.

That Deadly White Powder

The sugar in fruits naturally occurs. If you're eating a piece of fruit you're also getting the fiber, and all the other good things that come with it. It is the refined white crystallized sugar, high fructose corn syrup or any of the manmade sugary additives that end up in our foods and cause issues.

Sugar is four times more addictive than cocaine and it's more toxic than alcohol and tobacco. You're not hearing that fact in mainstream media. Sugar is everywhere. For most people the idea of completely giving up sugar completely is foreign. It is like any other addiction. If you're addicted to drugs, if you're addicted to alcohol, it's best if you step away from it completely and get it out of your environment.

It is up to you to decide if you have a problem with sugar. A lot of people have an addiction to sugar. They just don't know it. They think, "I want to eat this food all the time and I don't know why I can't give it up."

There is a reason. There are all kinds of additives in our foods in processed, packaged or fast food that get us addicted, to get our bodies to wanting those foods. Once we realize that we do better physically, mentally, emotionally and spiritually when we don't have those additives in those foods, we can take a step back and say, "I need to have a plan so that those foods and those ingredients aren't in my life."

Sugar is hiding in foods with high-glycemic indexes such as rice, potatoes and bread that transform into sugar in your body. You don't ordinarily think that a potato or a dish of rice is a sugar-creating food.

The Glycemic Index is basically a ranking of carbohydrates on a scale of 0 to 100. That scale is measures the extent to which foods raise the blood sugar levels and how quickly that happens.

A lot of people are surprised that corn, rice and potatoes are high on the Glycemic Index. They convert into sugar once they're inside our bodies. You can go online and look up the Glycemic Index. Do your own research. There are several sites that describe foods that will raise your blood sugar more quickly than you might want to.

Fruit is a low glycemic food: apples, strawberries, peaches and pears. On the vegetable side, low glycemic vegetables are asparagus, broccoli, artichokes and Brussels sprouts. Those might be foreign foods to you, especially if you're living a fast-paced life and you're used to eating fast food, but those are the foods that your body is going to like a lot. That is fuel for your body.

How to Kick the Sugar Habit

Here's how you can make better choices and get away from those sugary foods.

1. **Clear the sugar out of your house and read labels.** If you pick up a food that has a label on it, read the ingredients. Remember when you're in the grocery store and when you're in your own home to read the ingredients. Sugar is hidden in a lot of different things. It's usually words that end in O-S-E like sucrose and glucose.

    Clear it out of the cabinets. If it's not around you, you can't eat it. At work that means don't have a big container of chocolate sitting on the edge of your desk. Get that stuff away from you. Get it out of your car.

2. **Also avoid processed junk food and drink plenty of water to clean your system out.** Eat more vegetables and eat more protein. Eating protein is a good thing to do even if you're vegan or vegetarian. You don't have to eat meat. You can get protein from

beans, legumes and even from vegetables like spinach. Eat protein and foods that will fuel your body and keep your glycemic index from spiking.

3. **Get support.** Find a health coach and a buddy. Go through this process together. Stopping sugar and changing the way you look at food is a process. It's not a one week you're doing this and then you go back to what I used to do. It's a lifelong plan and you will adjust it as you have life changes.

CHAPTER 19

Tackling Wellness for Success

Building on what I covered in the previous chapter, in this last chapter, I explore the concept of a wellness lifestyle. What goes into that? It is a long-term lifestyle that is not limited to diet or eating plans. It's involves mindset to make a healthy well-balanced lifestyle happen long term on your terms. Being healthy is vital for business success.

Count Your Chemicals

Count your chemicals, not your calories. If you wouldn't give it to your child or pet, why give it to yourself? It is that simple. If you wouldn't feed something that you think is unhealthy or trash to those who you care about, then why on earth would you care any less for your own health and eat carelessly?

You don't give an infant pizza or a lot of processed food and all that junk that you can't even understand.

We've made it hard. It really is simple. If you count your chemicals, which makes you become aware of what you're eating, you can literally add life to your years. Calories are easy to account for. They come and go depending on what we eat. It's the chemicals in those calories that stay for the long term and cause permanent damage and constant inflammation. Those are things obviously of greater concern for your long-term health. It is true that you are what you eat, so when you start to become mindful of what you're consuming then your liver and your gut will reward you with many healthy well-balanced years.

I know a lot of people say, "I don't even know what to look for. I don't even know where to start". Look at your labels when you're out shopping. Even if you don't know what it is when you're first starting out if you don't understand it, it's probably not a bad idea to just put it down on the shelf.

Just because it says natural doesn't necessarily mean that it's as healthy for you as you should be looking for. The natural organic industry is a multibillion dollar industry, so of course they're going to try and change the labels. You need be careful because a lot of them look natural and they will put it in the organic natural section.

Check EWG.com. It's an unbiased group called "Environmental Working Group" and they will tell you about a chemical. They will tell you if it's a carcinogen, if it's an inflammatory, if you should completely avoid it in foods or body products.

Yield Signs

A yield sign helps you to combat the overwhelm and misinformation around health and wellness. It should make you stop, drop and roll. Stop picking up that pretty package box of food. Drop it back on the shelf and roll the buggy to the natural organic section.

A yield sign makes you reconsider your daily choices in food, cosmetics, body products and cleaning products. It's applicable to anything that can be absorbed, inhaled or consumed. There's so much information and it can be overwhelming, yet honestly it is simple. Just get back to eating food you recognize. If you are not sure, Google is your friend to determine what's good and what's not good.

There are some awesome apps you can put on your phone to scan packages and SKU numbers at the stores. They will tell you what's in it, if it's good for you and all sorts of information. There are a lot of resources to help you while you're shopping, while you're trying to develop a healthier lifestyle and eating plan.

Yield Signs Revealed

1. **If it sounds too good to be true, it is.** There's no one diet pill or workout plan that's going to work for everything that you feel is out of balance. You will see some new eating plan, supplement, or diet pill and the advertising copy makes it seems like this is the answer to everything you think you have going wrong with your life. Sadly, it's not going to work for everybody.

The same plan will never work. It might work great for your mom, your girlfriend or your neighbor and it's not going to be as effective for you. If it sounds too good to be true, it is. Consider what you want to rebalance in your health or wellness.

- "What are you willing to do right now?"
- "What have you done in the past?"
- "What are you willing to do for the future?"

Have you ever bought a gym membership that you did not use? For some, high intensity exercise causes more damage and inflammation. When you discover your body type and your traits, you will be able to develop a plan of wellness that works for *you*.

Yes, you can have foods you love. There are also ways to change up those foods, make them healthier and still taste as good if not better without all the harmful ingredients. You might have to do a little bit of work, but it's worth it in the long run. When your gut is happy, that will add years to your life. That's what everyone really strives for. No one gets to the end of their life wishing they had more money. It's always better health and more time. If it sounds too good to be true, stop a minute and reevaluate what's best for you. That's the best way to add years to your life.

2. **Make a decision about what you're wanting. Is it a quick fix or is it a lifestyle change?** A lot of what you see on the market is a quick fix. Ask yourself, "What am I looking to achieve?" "Is it a quick change for a temporary timeframe if you have an event?"

    If it's a long-term change to where you can start living your healthiest version of you, create a vision boards. You can't achieve these goals with a quick fix. Are you building a legacy in your business? Are you interested in building a legacy to leave to your children? You can't do that unless you create a lifestyle change if you have habits that you need to change.

    Nothing great happens without some work. You must put work into everything. Be prepared to make changes a little bit of time to reset and have your best life come to fruition.

    Over the age of 30 obviously our metabolism starts to change; our digestive enzymes start to decrease, and it can take up to a year to lose those last 10 pounds and keep it off. Evaluate if you want something temporary or are you looking to create the greatest change. Stop, reevaluate and become mindful of what it is that is in your best health interest.

3. **Is it chemical or is it natural?** There are some things that will say "natural" and they really aren't, so you must pay attention to your labels. The liver is the most fantastic detox organ that we have until we

eat a lot of processed foods laden with chemicals. By choosing foods that have ingredients that you can pronounce and understand, you're giving your liver the chance to do what it needs to do to provide you with sustainable energy so that you feel better, so you can do better. Whatever you put in your body and on your body helps your liver keep you lean. Keeping it clean will keep you lean.

Micro Habits

A micro-habit for me is literally just a very simple step that you're willing to put into place every day that eventually turns into a lifestyle. Take one little thing whatever it is for you. For example, when I realized how many calories I was consuming by drinking chai tea latte, I switched to unsweetened passion tea.

What are your goals and what do you want to achieve? Write down the things that are the best for you and maybe some things that aren't so good. What are you willing to put into place today, continue tomorrow and Friday, and even do it on the weekends?

It's by taking those little steps slowly over time that leads to a less stressful life and long-term success.

It is literally the *starting* that stops most people because they just don't know where to start. Instead of thinking I have all this stuff I must do or get out, no, you don't. You have one little thing you got to worry about today and maybe one little piece of movement to add in. Just do that and be happy with yourself. Celebrate it and the next day we will add something else in. The next thing you know those micro-habits just created an entirely new sustainable lifestyle.

Now you have reached the end of your journey with this book, and I hope I've given you tips, strategies and insights to help you grow your LNC skills. Are you ready to go deeper? Let's talk about your business and how I might be able to assist you. Set up a time to talk at: **http://LNC.tips/gethelp**.

And please, write a review on Amazon for this book. It will greatly help me and the book. I've given you instructions on the next page. It is easy.

Consider Writing a Review

When you enjoy a book, it is a natural desire to tell others about it. Amazon.com provides a way to share your thoughts and I invite you to write a book review. It is easy. Here are tips:

1. After going to the link below on Amazon.com, the first thing you are asked to do is to **assign a number of stars** to the book you think matches your opinion of the book.

2. Create a **title** for the review. This can be a simple phrase, like "Awesome guide." If you are not sure what to say, look at the titles of other book reviews.

3. It is easiest to write the book in a **word processor** and then paste it into Amazon.com Your word processor will pick up typos before your review goes public.

4. Write the review as if you were **talking to another person** – you are – a person who comes to Amazon.com and is considering buying this book.

5. Include a description of what you found **most helpful**. Was it an idea, chapter, tip? Share that with the readers.

6. Next you may want to write **who you think would most benefit** from this book. Is it for beginners? Or is it more appropriate for some- one with experience with this topic?

7. What if you have something **negative** to say about the book? You may always reach me at patiyer@ legalnursebusiness.com to suggest changes in the book.

8. If you include negative feedback in the review, keep a positive perspective rather than attack the author.

Here are some sample phrases:

- While overall the book was good, I would change it by. . .

- I don't think this book is right for. . .

- I would improve this book by. . .

Before you hit save, **read everything over one more time**. Authors and readers appreciate book reviews and they get easier to write with time. Go to this link on Amazon.com to write your review.

Also please email me at **patiyer@legalnursebusiness.com** when you have posted your review.

Thank you,

Pat Iyer